6 Steps to Integrated Scl

SAP-Primavera Integration Made Easy

The only guide you will need to get that job done!

Comprehensive - Authoritative - Realistic

By Berthold Kastel

www.cei-corp.com

Publishers Cataloging-in-Publication Data

Kastel, Berthold.
6 steps to the integrated schedule : SAP-Primavera integration experience made easy / Berthold Kastel – Sarasota, Fl. : Competitive Edge International, c2014
p. ; cm
ISBN: 978-0-9741808-9-2
Includes bibliographical references and index.
1. Project management—Automation. 2. Project management—Computer programs. 3. Organizational effectiveness. 4. Information Technology. I. Title.

2014919710

First Edition, Publication Date: January 2015

"A book about SAP-Primavera Integration?
To be fair, I'd rather read Lee Child."

Keith Hogben

"I would rather still be surfing and playing golf."

Shane Mitchell

CONTENTS

Preface

I will not hold back here. Sometimes I may be too direct for your liking, but that is how I define the purpose of this book. I assume you prefer openness and straight talk, peppered with specific and real examples and experiences, over general talk and vague statements.

This is the real deal.

By following my advice I aim to help you stop wasting days, weeks and months, cut down on meetings, emails and circular discussions, and save you hundreds of thousands of dollars, or even more.

Above all I want you to become a more competitive business and a more capable adaptive enterprise that is more ready for the challenging demands of our rapidly changing networked world.

Let's do it!

Bert Kastel

Boise, Idaho
November 2014

Who Do I Think You Are?

This is a practical guide. It shares lots of knowledge, hands-on tips and lists, and tidbits of real-life experience that I gathered and am sharing in little stories and references. I will be talking directly to you, and in general not use the third person. As you will quickly discover I will also not hold back with my professional assessment, or even outright judgment.

My hope is that this brings a rather dry subject better to life and makes for a more interesting read. You may discover yourself agreeing or arguing with me. It does not matter as long as either one happens and you don't just doze off...

So who do I think you are?

Business Process Owner.

You are a business process owner with a specific pain point. You want to get a hold of your schedule and cost, standardize processes and implement a tool to keep improving on them, provide more meaningful data to project managers, empower schedulers and planners without letting them off the hook with respect to the ERP backend.

You may come more from the SAP or more from the Primavera side, but you definitely have a basic understanding of both. You like reporting and scheduling in Primavera P6, and see P6 as a much easier-to-use tool than SAP, but you know that without back-end integration its value is limited.

You instinctively see the benefits of the integration. Your initial analysis of tools on the market has made you confident that this is not all too bad of an exercise, although you have some minor doubts because there are quite a few stories out there hinting at complexities that are not immediately obvious.

Technical Owner - IT.

You are representing IT and are tasked with delivering the integration of SAP with Primavera. Somebody dumped this on you and while you have mature SAP capabilities, yourself or in your organization, your exposure to Primavera has been sporadic at best.

You are confident in the overall capabilities of your people and of your organization, although you feel somewhat hampered by this lack of Primavera experience. Since you know SAP and have delivered interfaces to the business before, you are fairly confident that this isn't too much of a challenge, as long as you get proper guidance and training.

Consultant or System Integrator.

You are tasked with implementing improved business capabilities for the client, by implementing or tweaking their SAP PS or PM modules, or Primavera, or by being responsible for the overall solution. While you understand the business and at least a large part of the SAP or Primavera business applications, you are not really an integration expert.

Your instinctive reaction is to look at this as a manageable exercise and you feel confident in your ability to understand and define business requirements. However, there is this vague feeling of Primavera, and definitely of SAP EPC or other integration tools, being a bit of a black box. Overall your going-in position is that with some help from a technical person or EPC consultant this should not be too difficult of a task.

Unless you have tried before, of course...

Project Manager.

You are tasked with managing the implementation of this project. Initially it was sold to you as a straightforward case, but the deeper you dig the more you realize that there is a high number of moving parts involved, technically and functionally, and involving a number of contractors and skills that do not always naturally play well with each other.

You are anxious to deliver and are looking for guidance to quickly get in calm waters by eliminating the unknown unknowns, addressing the known unknowns, and tackling the known knowns.

Introduction

This book contains the most comprehensive overview and most condensed summary of real-life and relevant information required to integrate schedules for the management of complex projects, and to successfully deliver SAP-Primavera projects. Yes, follow the six steps outlined herein and my specific and detailed advice - and you *will* succeed.

It is a practical guide. You will find explanations, lists, encouraging and cautionary tales, logical questions, and overall lots of context and details about processes, functionality, features, technology, architecture and usability.

My Motivation.

My frequent interaction with large corporations and organizations motivates me to do that. Let's look at the following example.

About five years ago I went to a client in Korea to conduct an integration workshop. Chances are you have used their products at some point in the past few years. This is a very renowned company considered world leading in a number of industries, from consumer products to industrial facilities and the delivery of large-scale services. One of their specialties is the delivery of complex projects.

To my big surprise, however, they had a very valid reason to invite me: Their project management tools and processes were what seemed like an amalgamation of disjointed products and transactions. Managing projects involved a large number of manual steps to align multiple levels of schedules and plans. Many of the tools used were PC based, like MS Project, Excel or Primavera, others were server-based like SAP PS or more recent versions of Primavera.

What was striking is how globally competitive they were, despite their project management tools and processes being blatantly insufficient at so many levels. This organization almost tangibly oozed with a potential for value, cost-savings, efficiency gains, risk reduction, and process improvements.

It took years before they were ready to take the next step, though, and this delay must have been really costly to them.

I always wonder why companies sometimes hold on with taking the right and obvious steps in such a strategic area as project management. This is how corporate strategies get executed, how business practices and capabilities are improved and world-class products and services delivered.

So let me help in the process.

My Background.

During the past 15 years I have contributed to building complete SAP-Primavera integration tools. Additionally I have been personally involved in a large number of implementations. I have conducted over one hundred workshops, seminars, presentations, and analyses of requirements relating to organizational project management solutions in general, and specifically to SAP-Primavera integration. I have read many dozens of requirement documents, produced a large number myself, and given an innumerable number of presentations and demonstrations.

This books references personal experiences from and with SAP-Primavera integration projects on every continent and in all major world regions, from all regions of the U.S. to Canada, South America, East Asia, Australia, Africa, the Middle East, and Europe:

- Refineries, petrochemical and chemical plants
- Large oil & gas companies, established conglomerates and new joint ventures
- Engineering and Construction companies, from medium-sized construction to large-scale delivery and make-to-order
- Service organizations and general contractors, in multiple industries and with varying skills

- Utilities, of various sizes and specialization
- And many more

I have been involved in depth with all of these, with their processes and challenges. Sometimes I had to dive down into code, although most of the time I had the privilege to work with some of the World's premier experts in project management related enterprise integration, Angus Scott-Knight and Shane Mitchell, doing that hard job for me.

I have worked with various technologies, ranging from custom built ones with languages and tools like Java or even ColdFusion, and using bTalk, to applications like Intech and Pipeline Project Transporter, while also having contributed to or worked with Impress, smaller interfaces, and custom solutions built by consultancies and product companies.

All these SAP-Primavera integration projects succeeded, although some others never went beyond an initial analysis or POC. Not all of them had been smooth, though, and these experiences are as important as the smooth successes. When SAP-EPC came out our team performed the first independent implementations of that product. Talk about challenges!

With all the exposure to various technologies, I never looked at SAP-Primavera integration as a primarily technical exercise. It is a business process improvement exercise, and is to be seen in the context of and as a major contributing factor to increasing an organizations overall project management maturity. Even more, it determines one's ability to effectively execute and deliver corporate strategies.

My Contribution.

The contents of this book, my assessments, and my recommendations incorporate all of the above.

It makes me sometimes feel like a real expert, but one who at the same time realizes ever more the many instances where his knowledge, experience and skills fall short. It makes me believe that the real experts are you who work in the project management field doing your specific jobs. I can bring knowhow and perspectives and experiences, and bring all of that together. You need to apply it.

A (almost true) Story

So let me tell you a story...

Ashna and Dave, representing IT and business of a large multinational corporation are tasked with finding and implementing a solution to integrate SAP and Primavera. Their PMO has declared it a priority to develop and implement standardized project management processes, using the "best of breed" tools of SAP and Primavera.

Digging into some corporate history, they realize that there had been a couple of attempts to achieve the same. At that time, the project did in one case not get off the ground, and in the other case was it abandoned after an ineffective proof of concept.

The earlier try rendered a number of technical doubts, but also revealed that neither SAP nor Primavera processes were mature and standardized enough. Most Primavera users were still working with the PC-based product, not even using the client-server based Primavera Enterprise. There even was a strong countercurrent in IT to further explore the use of MS Project. Anyway, at that time Impress was the only interface product with a noticeable footprint in the market. Putting all of that together, rightly or wrongly it was considered way too expensive, horrendous to support, and with questionable performance.

A few years later the initiative was revived when Oracle bought Primavera and with it Inspire, a related integration product that used SAP's enterprise application integration (EAI) platform XI under the hood. Oracle stated clearly that integration into SAP was a priority, and they pushed their product. Over some strong opposition, Inspire was picked over some more nimble competitors because of its affiliation with Primavera.

This time the endeavor went further, reaching the stage of a proof of concept (POC). The wish of the user community was to keep as much functionality out of SAP, and to drive the corporate project management standards using Primavera as the easier-to-use product with a much larger and well-established user basis. Building that process using Inspire proved to be way more complicated than anticipated, though. Huge gaps of functionality were discovered in several areas.

Even more, the little integration that was actually performed during the POC was awfully slow with a data transfer rate of no more than several hundred activities per hour. That was not nearly enough for either capital or turnaround projects with tens of thousands of activities. The interface seemed buggy and it was decided that everything just was way too complicated and risky. So this second attempt was aborted also.

The third time will be the charm, everybody hopes. The PMO has clearly stated that SAP and a recent release of Primavera P6 will be the enterprise project management products of choice. Project management is to be standardized across the enterprise, integrated into SAP budgeting processes, financials and procurement, while Primavera will be the scheduling and reporting engine of choice. Further details are to be discovered through the course of the project.

The approximate timeline is set fairly aggressively, as "by the end of the year". Even though it is a big company, this time "by the end of the year" does not sound anymore like "by the end of a year". A failure to deliver anything but an integrated world-class project management solution absolutely does not seem to be an option anymore.

As Ashna and Dave are looking for interfaces, they are searching the Internet, ask in-house schedulers and planners, some consultants, and SAP and Oracle directly. They already discovered that the old time Impress product did not seem to be totally dead after all and that Oracle-Primavera's Inspire is still around also, with cool marketing literature on the web.

Pipeline Software's Transporter product remained a clear niche player. The biggest news is that people returning from a recent SAP user conference keep mentioning SAP Enterprise Project Connection (EPC) as the tool of choice strongly pushed by SAP. "Lots of out-of-the-hoc mappings supported by SAP" definitely sounds appealing.

The stakeholders have varying concerns. Schedulers don't want big and complicated SAP processes stifle their ability to support project schedules. SAP users responsible for budgeting, financial control and procurement keep wondering why anybody would even bother with something as strange as Primavera. After all, SAP's PS and PM modules have all project management functionality one could wish for, don't they?

IT does not want another integration platform in-house and prefers to use their investment in SAP PI, although related stories there are not too encouraging to predict a quick win. Anyway, they also wonder why they could not connect these applications themselves, using "web services" or something like that. Some inside the organization point at past failures, although that was at a time when the iPad was not even released yet and Vladimir Putin was still President of Russia. Okay he still is, but you know what I mean, that could have been ages ago.

With this in mind Ashna and Dave now start their journey to deliver a solution. They start out with a short list of contacts and are making some phone calls.

If nothing of the above sounds familiar, stop right now. Pick up a good action novel from John Gilstrap or Greg Rucka, or Kissinger's "World Order" and enjoy - these are great reads and you will get more out of them than from this book.

If something does ring a bell with you, though, turn the page and get going. There are six major steps on how to integrate SAP with Primavera. Follow these instructions, and keep the 8 Myth-Busters and 15 Pitfalls in mind.

Then you will succeed.

I will tell you exactly how to get the job done.

Setting the Stage: SAP and Primavera

Did you catch my lie in the title? Nothing ever is "easy" when it comes to SAP. Or Oracle, for that matter, and Primavera is an Oracle product.

But don't blame me, at least you started reading and that is what I wanted to make you do. You will get value out of it. This is the one-stop-shop for information about SAP-Primavera Integration.

For the purpose of the challenge addressed by this book, the SAP and Primavera applications are not too dissimilar. We are talking about applications that facilitate project management, whether in the context of capital projects, make-to-order projects, maintenance, outages, or delivery of complex services. The main objects look alike in many ways:

- Primavera projects and SAP projects
- Primavera WBS and SAP WBS
- Primavera activities and SAP activities (or operations)
- Primavera labor resources and SAP labor resources (i.e. work centers or individuals)
- Primavera relationships and SAP relationships

And so on. Mapping similar fields in similar applications should not be too challenging of a task.

How difficult can that be?

Well, it is not too difficult at all - if you know what you are doing and why, set realistic parameters, use the right people and the right tools, design the solution well, and follow the right approach. Doing that turns one of the inherently most complex tasks in the enterprise project management world into a fairly straightforward exercise.

And this is what the book is about. Not more and not less.

Follow the advice herein and you will succeed and significantly improve the ability of your organization to effectively and efficiently deliver results through projects. And since these results typically reflect change, and change is supposed to improve things - this book will help you make the world a better place.

Why keep ambitions too modest: I am just talking, it is you who has to deliver...

1.

WHERE? DEFINE STRATEGIC GOALS

Where do you want to go?

The integrated project schedule is about making you more competitive through more effective execution.

Here is the situation today, in our world in the 21st century. You are under competitive pressure all the time. The world is changing rapidly. You need to adapt quickly to different market situations, regulatory requirements, customer demands, cost pressures, competitors, and technologies.

So what do you do? What do you do if you have a limited budget, a limited number of people, if you have only limited time and resources available?

You prioritize.

Above all you try to come up with a coherent strategy ensuring that whatever you are pursuing is in line with your strategic objectives as an organization. So when you decide to invest money, time and effort in developing new products, it needs to fit into that context. When you improve your capital investment, when you explore or expand your production base, when you change your organization to make it more fit, when you introduce new technologies or processes into your organization, when you upgrade your corporate infrastructure - all this needs to be aligned with your corporate strategies.

These corporate strategies are expressed in initiatives and are evaluated using performance indicators that often do or should involve aspects of quality, risk, cost, and all kinds of benefits and long-term strategic and technical considerations.

And then these strategic initiatives will need to get "done".

The way they are executed, always, is through projects. And this is what I am talking about here.

I am talking about enterprise projects in a rapidly changing environment, to help you to adapt and deliver on strategic objectives that are defined and need to be measured and managed during the implementation of these projects.

But here I go, talking in this book about integration of schedules, of data. Does moving data help you achieve your corporate objectives? I say "of course", since the impact of integration goes far beyond technology. In reality it is not about moving some similar data between similar kinds of systems. It is about **execution**. It is about enabling you to provide the information to these KPIs that you are basing your project and corporate strategic decisions on.

Not doing that means inefficiently and ineffectively executing strategies and in the extreme even possibly putting the future of the organization at risk.

Without integration you cannot know whether information is correct. Information from the bottom cannot trickle up, top down directions cannot be communicated effectively, and there are no quality feedback loops.

All you know is "something".

Therefore I will not talk about implementing a software product. I will describe how to make sure that a stage-gate process can work that measures scope, cost, and time, as well as progress and performance levels, of these arguably most critical efforts for the future of your organization. It ensures that these projects will be implemented effectively and efficiently.

The contribution of linking these systems is to provide seamlessly integrated information to the people executing corporate strategies. Better information, more information, the right information faster to the right people at the right time.

This is what the integrated schedule is about, not the moving of some data.

The Importance of "Strategy Alignment"

Let's be realistic and honest to ourselves, upfront.

Or in other words: What is the best way to get started?

A few months ago I received an email from a large, and in my understanding well-run, business located in the Middle East. They asked me whether I would be interested in implementing a solution between their SAP ECC and external scheduling applications.

After I said "yes" I received a formal Request for Proposal (RFP). It was full of detailed commercial parameters and conditions that clearly reflected capable input from a procurement department. However, some of the functional scope elements expressed therein were extremely vague, unrealistic or incomplete, and most of the technical context was not addressed and specified. Upon a review I gave feedback on the document, pointing out obvious inconsistencies and giving examples for scope and technical aspects to be included.

Within days I had a new version in my hand, incorporating most of my comments. I should have been happier because the client obviously listened to me, but mostly my concerns were accentuated. It became obvious that the company had not sufficiently thought through and specified critical project parameters. My input mentioned issues but could not possibly have sufficiently addressed them.

The project risk was too big, so I had to respectfully decline my further contribution to the endeavor at this time.

I wished that the above were a rare exception. Unfortunately, however, I am encountering this quite often. Clients rushing into a SAP-Primavera integration project without properly addressing many or even most strategic and tactical aspects that ensure project success. Businesses greatly underestimating the complexity of the endeavor.

Often they realize that they have shortcomings. Then, however, they don't address them in a formal manner upfront, but assume they can push those into the project implementation effort. The first time they approach outside experts is during a procurement effort.

That normally is too late. It is all backwards.

Almost all RFPs I have seen, and almost all conversations and demos I had been involved with, are missing key design decisions. They also usually leave out substantial solution components, and fall short in their description of key functional and technical specifications. Businesses are confident about their IT department's capabilities, and they have one or the other person in-house who has been involved with some form of SAP-Primavera integration application, or even with a project that used and implemented such.

Often they look for an "EPC Consultant" or something to that effect, to help them get pointed in the right direction. How difficult can it be, after all, with a handful of vendors describing how wonderfully easy things get nowadays. Therefore they claim that all they need is a variation of what they found out about ready-to-install templates, give or take a few minor tweaks.

This sounds like a perfect checklist for my "8 Deadly Sins" list of Myths surrounding SAP-Primavera Integration.

To prevent the above, I suggest a formal multi-week process of strategic evaluations, alignment and clarification. Such an effort should not lean primarily on the vendors of technical integration platforms, but combine internal and external experts tasked with a realistic and mostly vendor-agnostic definition of key project parameters.

As an optional subsequent step, a proof-of-concept (POC) can shed high-value additional light on process scope, functional, and technical considerations.

The first question to answer is "Why am I doing this?"

Know Your Pain-Points: Why am I doing this?

Before kicking off a project to integrate SAP and Primavera, be clear about why you are doing it. Being upfront about the key pain points and goals helps evaluating and defining parameters for the delivery of the solution.

Integrating SAP and Primavera is not about mapping a few similar fields between two similar project management applications. A WBS ID becomes a WBS ID, an activity becomes an activity, a relationship becomes a relationship, percent complete is percent complete - how difficult can it be?

Yes, that would indeed be rather simple, but the reality is that an integrated schedule lays the foundation for KPIs that feed into portfolio management, continuous process improvement, internal or external benchmarking, effective cost management, earned value management, detailed project progress reporting, and an overall better ability to support similar projects and train personnel. All that leads to more efficiencies and effectiveness - directly adding to the bottom line while laying the foundation to reduce risks and improve quality.

How is that for a start?

Since it is not primarily a software implementation effort, don't treat it as such. The integrated schedule is a business solution that should provide tangible results for the enterprise. These results should improve the bottom line, lower risks, enforce proven processes, and improve the safe delivery of quality products. If not, why do it?

Typical pain points go beyond inconveniences or double work. They are business issues, like:

- Inconsistent schedules
- Missing of critical information

- Inability to control costs properly
- Inefficient use of resources
- Lack of earned value, forecasting, and reporting capabilities

They result in missing of deadlines and budgets, in dissatisfying project performance, and poor quality of deliverables. Combined with the inability to effectively benchmark and perform postmortem analyses, this perpetuates inefficiencies in delivering repetitive processes. Or in English: Project results are all over the place because one cannot see what went right or wrong.

The typical goals of an integration solution address the above. They lay the foundation to establish proven standardized processes, benchmarking capabilities, the tracking of KPIs, and establish the use of more advanced and capable project management.

There are variations of the main pain points, though.

Outages and Turnarounds.

Here, time is money, almost literally. Not just the out-of-pocket costs, but mainly the opportunity costs of downtime can be very significant. At the same time, though, too much time pressure can lead to mistakes and affect safety. The main driver for the integration solution is then the need for frequent updates multiple times a day, the ability to manage execution and sign-off on inspections, and to provide enough data for a thorough postmortem analysis and benchmarking with similar events or locations in your business.

I have seen this at a large Canadian oil and gas client that needed to update their schedule twice a day, typically working 12-hour shifts, and at a South African utility that needed to update their schedule up to four times a day. In both cases the business driver is to shorten the actual outages, get production up safely but also as quickly as possible, and thus minimize lost revenue and overall outage costs.

The interaction between planning and execution was most clearly expressed to me during an evaluation of outage management processes at a Californian utility. The outage manager described to me the interaction between safety and an integrated schedule. When I asked how long their schedule, planned over two years, lasts in the heat of the battle during an outage, the answer was, "it sometimes lasts until the second day". And then? Then feedback loops take too long and the managing becomes "ad-hoc", "off-the-seat-of-one's-pants", "winging it". Safety is then maintained, and execution ensured, by multiplying the numbers of people involved.

It does not have to be that way. A decade later I was able to help the above-mentioned South African's deliver a workable integrated turnaround management solution. Similarly, at a Dutch petrochemical plant I observed how they design their solution to actively focus on involving all responsible parties in execution. After a very detailed and disciplined outage planning process, the schedule remains the execution management tool. They create accountability and ownership by providing the various teams with high-quality to do lists, and driving inspectors' sign-off directly back into the schedule.

On the other hand the outage manager at a Louisiana-based Chemical plant expressed the issue at hand even more pointedly. He told me, "Primavera, SAP, MS Project, whatever - my men know what to do so we don't need to let the scheduling tool get in their way."

This thinking is what one wants to overcome, by developing the trust into abilities of a schedule to provide efficiencies beyond one single event. That then results in a working schedule for better performance in the future.

Do you think these events can shave off a few days of their outages schedule? Absolutely. The savings? Millions.

What does it require? High performance through-put, an execution-driven use of Primavera based on data output from a disciplined planning process in SAP, to increase safety, provide benchmark data, and accountability and thus performance improvements that lead to very substantial savings.

Capital or Make-to-Order Projects.

Now we go to the other side of the spectrum. Time and data volume often is not quite as much of an issue, but control of complex schedules and cost that often are planned in a decentralized manner. Projects may consist of multiple levels, with one Master Schedule relating to the high-level Structure in SAP, while more detailed projects are either owned by contractors, or treated as lower-level component based schedules managed internally as separate projects.

A Canadian oil company does the first one. They host Primavera in the cloud and load high-level Cost Breakdown Structures as a high-level WBS. This they then break out into more details and manually incorporate contractor progress feedback. Since SAP sends over cost information, the schedulers are able to pull realistic earned value data out of the integrated Primavera master schedule.

If you know about the Aerospace and Defense industry, then you know that this is somewhat similar to how they manage their 'system of systems" approach to the delivery of complex projects. Often one does at the beginning of the project not yet know what technologies will exist and will be integrated a few years down the road.

One of our customers in that industry manages such complexity using multiple component schedules as separate projects, rolling up to the master schedule. Again, only a portion of the master schedule is integrated with SAP. The main pain point here is the integrated schedule itself, and a secondary goal is to lay the foundation for future earned value and cost based controls.

Both customer examples were mainly about usability, or lack thereof in SAP, and the integration of lower-level schedules into a master schedule for more effective progress and status controls. Therefore both companies try to pull as much high-level data as possible from SAP into Primavera, and then let end users almost solely work in Primavera.

A Philosophical Challenge: Bridging Continental Divides

Let's face it; what we really often are doing when integrating SAP and Primavera is to bridge ocean-wide divides. On the one side is the powerful and overwhelming ugly machine, on the other side the cool and beautiful work of art enabling real people to contribute in the real world. I leave it up to you to match them up.

As funny as it may be, of course that image is nonsense when looking at many of the specific facts.

Still, there is a kernel of truth in the above, and since perception is to a large degree reality it does not hurt keeping the above in mind when looking at the task at hand.

The main implementation challenge is to bridge the above seemingly huge gap philosophically and conceptually. When looking at what each application is doing, where shortcomings are, and what would theoretically be required to overcome them, oceans become rivers and intuitively we already see many places to build bridges that connect and make everybody stronger.

Let's get more specific about this poetic sentence: A main reason for Primavera being perceived as easier to use is that it is not a complete project management tool, while a main reason for SAP being perceived as difficult to use is that it does too many things for too many people and too many situations.

So why not enhance Primavera by pulling relevant project management-related data from SAP, do the magical calculations and analyses in P6 at a more meaningful level, and then return more relevant data to where SAP can pick it up and link it back to the rest of the enterprise. Nimbleness where required, power and complexity where necessary, and everybody is better off.

Yeah, why not? Interests aligned. Value created. Bottom-line improved.

That's what we really do when integrating these tools.

A Look at Primavera.

From a project management perspective, Primavera schedulers and planners see themselves as closer to the real action of where much of the project work gets done. They come up with the specific list of work tasks to be completed by specific people to produce specific deliverables at a specific time. When tangible results are to be delivered somebody needs to tell real people what to do and the source of that information often is Primavera.

Or is it? I will argue that the calculation of this information is done in Primavera, and its presentation, but that Primavera rarely is the real source. A simple thought exercise makes my point.

- The deliverables need to be defined corporate-wide by linking them to corporate strategic goals with tangible KPIs. The tool for that is an informal portfolio management process, or a formal portfolio management tool, like SAP PPM.
- The specific people need to be employed and managed and paid for internally, or procured externally. The first requires a human resource management tool like SAP HR/HCM, the second a service procurement tool like the one being part of the SAP MM module.
- The materials and tools and pieces of equipment need to be procured and provided through a tool like, again, SAP MM. Sometimes they are to be produced internally, managed by a tool equivalent to SAP PP, or linked to SAP MRP to determine what needs to be bought and what comes from a warehouse.
- Money needs to be made available through a corporate budgeting process, and more specifically by optimizing corporate-wide cash flow management. The SAP FI and CO modules, sometimes also SAP IM, provide this capability.
- Some work priorities and specific scope considerations may need to be defined by a corporate planning process, like maintenance cycles of equipment and functional locations (using tools like SAP PM), or may be triggered

through corporate sales processes and related milestones (using tools like SAP SD).

Please note that none of the above can be derived out of Primavera itself, but that any company running SAP as their ERP application has most or all of these components in place. On top of that procurement and financial management go all the way around. And I did not even go into the details of project stock.

Then note that procurement people in SAP don't need to second guess time anymore, to determine when materials, people, or cash needs to be provided. That key piece of optimizing information comes from SAP. And on top of that we can reconcile what is planned with actuals, and measure progress through earned value calculations based on real data.

Now that sounds like the real deal of SAP-Primavera integration!

The PMBOK and more...

The Project Management Book of Knowledge () of the Project Management Institute (PMI) lists 9 Knowledge Areas: Scope, Time, Cost, Human Resources, Procurement, Quality, Scope, Communication, and Integration. The quadruple constraint of project management lists Scope, Time, Cost, and Quality. As far as generic information goes, Primavera only is capable to provide a couple of these - Time Management, and maybe Scope Management. All other input will need to be fed manually or through interfaces.

However, when fed by SAP, schedulers can take Primavera's superior user friendliness and flexibility to not just do their job, but to do their job better. Both worlds are connected and better off.

That almost sounds like optimizing business by using the comparative advantages of various tools in a rational matter. Like economics!

The above is true, but it is not the whole truth. It leaves out a key piece, which is the fact that much of the information that the schedulers need does come from the ERP system.

The main arguments for using Primavera are user-friendliness and reporting capability. Only to a lesser degree it is about functionality. User-friendliness and reporting often blur powerfully into each other by allowing to interactively and quickly look at different views of data in a graphically appealing manner. What Primavera does do is to perform key and complicated portions of project management in a superior manner. To do this best, it needs help from SAP, though.

El Dorado vs. The Milking Cow

People need to work with each other to achieve the above-described integration and related strategic goals.

Since the internal and external teams are likely to interact with each other for the first time during the early design stage, here are two ways of how not to interact with each other... Some of the below is just part of the give-and-take during the early stage of a project, and luckily neither one is common as a persistent modus operandi.

Sometimes boundaries are crossed, though, to everybody's detriment. On the other side, reasonable sensitivity and extra effort to show mutual respect can not only prevent issues but develop informal or formal professional relationships that increase everybody's reputation and will render long-term benefits.

I call the two extremes the "Consulting El Dorado" vs. "The Milking Cow".

Consulting El Dorado...

"Let's get the door opened, then we can stick around this client for years - there is plenty of work and tons of money to be made."

Who has ever heard something like that? Unfortunately, statements like these still all-too-frequently burden the relationship between external consultant and client. The more consultants sell "time" instead of "solutions", the more likely one is to come across such thinking.

The statement itself may at times just be unfortunately phrased. Often it correctly reflects a client in dire need of help and an excellent match in complementary external skills that bring about significant value to a business. There is something to be said about skillful and experienced consultants having seen many different similar situations and being able to spread innovative approaches.

There also sometimes is arrogance and disdain speaking, seeing a client as a cash cow that can be milked long-term by adroitly playing the "political game". A good indicator of that can be if large IT organizations or systems integrators change seats and roles without much impact on the effectiveness of an organization. Sometimes that is even aided by a client's internal politics and short-term career objectives of key management.

...or The Milking Cow

I have also sometimes seen the reverse behavior. Clients milking consultants for all their know-how, without charge, trying to absorb as much knowledge and direction as possible on the cheap. Sales processes are an "excellent" way of achieving this, using questions about technical capabilities and implementation approaches and lessons learned and demonstrations to disguise the real intention to just get enough input to do most of the job themselves.

In the SAP-Primavera integration world this rarely can work, for a couple of reasons.

(1) SAP-Primavera integration know-how and skills are not commodities. They are among the highest-specialized skills of the enterprise application market, due to the natural process, functional, and technical complexities of the implementation. This grants the experts a strong position.

(2) It is usually quite obvious what is happening, and sets a controversial undertone. Even if customers and vendors manage to establish a formalized business relationship at

a later point in time, it is not a fully trusting one. Consultants will build higher contingencies for risk into their quotes, while customers may still wonder whether they could not have gotten implementations cheaper (and both are right!).

By all means use a "trust and verify" approach. Let them show you their capabilities, with live demos, describe challenges they encountered and how they resolved them, and talk to individual team members.

Then, however, treat your service provider as an integral member of the team and trust their capabilities and integrity. Align project success contractually, by defining fixed price milestones or limited time and expense-based engagements. Don't push too hard on the price and keep in mind that there is enough demand and skills are scarce. Be tough but fair.

Once the dimension of cost is right, common-sense validations look fine, focus on the value generated and not on cost. If you then push the service provider, do it by insisting on the highest levels of quality, explicitly stated in contracts or implied. Don't cheap out but let them give you a bit of extra.

One of the most heartening conversations I ever had in that respect was many years ago with British Petroleum. This was also in the context of an SAP-Primavera integration project. BP team members told me that price was not their main criterion when evaluating the solution. It just needed to be in a common sense ballpark. Quality of service, reputation, skills, tools, implementation approach, and the overall ability to deliver were what counted to them above all.

Due to the complexity of the implementation, **not** following a partnering approach between customers and suppliers risks project success and almost invariably introduces some increased measure of inefficiencies and tension. The fact that SAP-Primavera integration is not a commodity means that it is a small world. This alone is usually motivation enough for the consultant to deliver the best services possible.

Cost-Benefit Definition

Above I described a typical pain point in general terms. As important as that is, the expected benefits can be more tangibly expressed. Usually this is done financially. Before diving into the details of technical, functional, and business parameters, identify the cost benefit expected out of the endeavor.

Most likely corporate appropriation processes require some sort of cost-benefit analysis. How this is conducted provides one of the most meaningful guidelines for the other five steps. It helps being clear about and staying aware of whether an implementation is seen mainly as:

A. A value generating tool to improve overall project management maturity and therefore a key driver for the execution of corporate strategy;

B. A means to cut cost, e.g. by reducing downtime during industrial outages or improving schedule and cost performance on capital investment projects, or reducing risks; or

C. A sheer replacement of a previous manual process and to make life easier for schedulers.

Sometimes it is a combination of the above, which usually provides the most fruitful ground for high-value implementations. Let's look at each one more closely.

A Value Generating Tool

Reason A views the project as a corporate exercise of strategic value since it is a major stepping stone in enabling higher project management maturity across the business. This reflects the role that enterprise projects really are supposed to play, according to advanced principles of organizational project management. Here is how it goes, often also described as the major part of a portfolio management process:

During a corporate strategy enterprise, business strategies are broken down into initiatives and associated projects. These are evaluated based on pre-defined key performance indicators

(KPIs), and approved based on their relative contribution to help driving and achieving acknowledged corporate strategic goals.

Approved projects are formally authorized, receive a budget, and follow from that point on a stage-gate process considering key milestones and in-project evaluations and approvals to ensure that they live up to their KPIs.

In this context, this is not about integrating SAP and Primavera per se. This is about a strategic endeavor to provide the means to correctly perform projects, and to measure and evaluate key factors like scope, time, cost, and the management of internal and procured resources. It also is about a seamless flow of correct and relevant information to business users, independent of the application used.

Today's integrated world requires an enterprise adapt to change. The means to adapt is change itself, expressed in projects. The ability to properly plan, execute and evaluate projects is therefore one of the most strategic and highest-value initiative an organization can have in the 21st century.

In that context, this seemingly primitive task of transferring similar data between similar applications lays a critical foundation for the modern enterprise.

A Means to Cut Cost

Reason B can be related to (A) but often is sufficient as a justification by itself. The logic here is that substantial cost savings can be achieved shaving off project time, reducing project stock or delays due to late deliveries, optimizing cash flow, eliminating wasted resources, or identifying issues and discrepancies between progress reported versus planned and actual time spent.

A good example are turnarounds and outages, where production downtime often results in daily revenue reduction of millions of dollars, and where the costs of thousands of contractors can reach similar dimensions.

A typical industrial plant will then easily lose seven digits a day during the actual outage. The benefits of a tight integration of the project schedule (Primavera) into the financial, planning and procurement tool (SAP) can be expressed tangibly. Estimate the targeted performance improvement of the outage, expressed in numbers of days, and multiply it by your daily "number".

This also applies to other projects, like capital or make-to-order projects, where one can quantify performance expressed in targeted cost savings of certain cost components (e.g. Labor cost, warehouse), or risk reduction and related higher revenues or lower costs by sticking to delivery timelines.

Another indirect and related value that also is very substantial can also be quantified. It is that an integrated schedule based on standardized processes provides an excellent foundation for internal benchmarking. E.g., if you have 12 plants with a turnaround every three years, following a standardized and automated process, over the period of 10 years you can compare the performance of 100 turnarounds, identifying and spreading best practices, and discovering and eliminating deficiencies.

An integration project justified with the above is more tangible than scenario A. While the overall benefit for the corporation is likely to be less, it being tangible can be a great motivator to not skimp on the quality of the solution. It focuses the project team and it is easy to keep the context in perspective.

An Efficiency Tool

Reason C would be the equivalent to treating the SAP-Primavera integration project as a technical exercise, or the implementation of a technical interface. It is likely to imply a narrow and technocratic scope. The logic is to compare the implementation of a tool like EPC to the uploading and downloading of files, manual re-typing of detailed or summary data mainly during planning processes, or verbal communication per phone or email during project execution.

The cost benefits are evaluated by calculating hours of effort saved per project, or per month, for re-typing, phone calls, reconciliations, or fixing of errors. For a single location or major project one is hard-pressed to determine savings of more than a day or two a week. Extrapolating that over five years will even in countries with high labor cost rarely add up to more than $250,000. Counter that with costs for hardware, software licenses, support, and internal labor during the implementation, and the overall total cost of ownership (TCO) calculation leaves very little for a meaningful implementation project.

These values can get higher when such manual steps include the loading and transformation of schedules from third parties, as it frequently happens in projects with large numbers of contractors that own partial or component level schedules.

In any way, the challenge of such a narrow scope is that it becomes difficult to justify substantial investments. This leads to consistent pressure on the implementation team since expectations of the quality of the solution are rarely lowered, and it is difficult to get even the most necessary support in terms of manpower and systems.

Such a scope also is most likely to look at the task of integrating SAP and Primavera as mainly a software installation and subsequent mapping exercise.

Next Steps

Perform an "Early Design" or "Feasibility Analysis" that addresses and defines strategic and tactical pre-project parameters. This can then become the basis to address project logistics, the Statement of Work, and the Project Charter. Start with assembling a team consisting of at a minimum the following relevant skills and functions:

- SAP Basis System
- SAP Functionality (i.e. modules PS and/or PM)
- Primavera P6 Functionality
- Primavera P6 Technical Aspects (including API)
- Functional Processes to be addressed (e.g. Capital Project Management, Outage and Turnaround Management, Make-to-Order Projects), covering the complete project life cycle
- Corporate Project Management Standards (e.g. PMO)

- Network & Infrastructure Support

Identify and include (temporarily hire) outside experts with specific implementation experience covering all the above functions. Make sure they have broad and deep enough experience to add value by guiding through the definition of all 15 parameters described next.

Conduct an initial kickoff meeting to define the scope of the exercise, which in its essence covers the above mentioned 15 sets of questions. Limit the exercise to about 4 to 6 weeks. Perform some initial internal fact gathering and schedule a 3 to 5 day workshop to jointly review the questions.

Follow up with a document outlining all answers, and give everybody the opportunity to provide detailed feedback. Wrap up that job and now you are ready to move on to the core part of the implementation.

2.

WHY? SET REALISTIC TACTICAL PARAMETERS

Setting the Stage in One Month

Addressing the challenge does not require something totally new. A simple look at how other complex projects are approached provides a helpful guideline: Perform the equivalent of a feasibility study or early-stage design.

Its purpose is not just to financially compare costs vs. benefits, but also to outline general parameters for the delivery of your SAP-Primavera integration solution.

Define a mini-project in advance of even putting out a formal inquiry. Such an effort can be similar to a feasibility study. Short and crisp. Pull together all relevant stakeholders, and assemble a small team from the business, from IT, of functional SAP people, Primavera schedulers, planners, procurement, engineers, maintenance or turnaround managers. Complement this internal team with experts from the outside. Make sure it is a competent team that has done it all, not just one individual having been involved with a similar exercise a couple of years ago.

However, do not treat this like an open-ended invitation to define requirements or corporate standards. Treat it as an extension of what you already know if you have a Project Management Organization (PMO) or organizational equivalent.

Take a few weeks of time; 4 to 6 weeks should be enough. The goal is to address the questions listed below, to define strategic parameters, not to define detailed requirements or improve business processes. Should you not be able to perform the below within 4 to 6 weeks, you simply may not be ready yet.

Having been involved with or exposed to a relevant degree to far over 100 of the largest and most complex organizations of the world, I come to the conclusion that "they" (= the totality of their internal people) usually know best. They know what practices work best for them; they know how to structure and deliver their projects; they know the capabilities of their organizations. External consultants can facilitate requirements definitions, and help guide through standardization and change management processes, but that is mainly as an extension of internal teams. The original work has to be done by internal experts.

Outside experts do have their place, though, even and maybe particularly early on in the pre-project phase.

As strategically important as an integrated schedule can be, for an experienced team it is not complicated. The main challenge is in the unusually high number of moving parts technically, functionally, and process-wise, and the associated complexities. It is about getting the job done while ensuring quality and reducing risk.

To get there, pull everybody in one room, including outside experts. Have a budget for it. Not a huge one, but treat the value of what you are getting with the proper respect: It may be a go-no go decision or the definition of parameters and alignment of expectations that can add millions to the bottom line of your business, or prevent wasting everybody's time, money and nerves.

One final word: Treat the Early-Design Analysis also as an opportunity to feel out your experts, to validate your team in terms of expertise, capabilities, experience, tools, but also chemistry vis-a-vis each other. It is an excellent opportunity to do so at a time when the mutual risk is still low.

List of Parameters

Here is a list of the main parameters to be defined upfront, each of which I will address in more details later. It contains the necessary items for the early stages of a project. In itself it is not sufficient to replace the preparation of specification phase of an actual implementation project.

The list contains 15 items, which I grouped in three areas. If you are able to give me clear answers to these questions, I will be able to give you a realistic quote, and the likelihood of project success is almost guaranteed.

Technical Parameters

1. Integration Platform.
   Should one be used or not? How is it to be evaluated? What capabilities does it need to have?
2. Buy versus Build.
   To what degree are solution components to be purchased? When should the decision be made to build them yourself?
3. Supportability.
   To what degree do you expect to support the solution in-house?
4. Software Versions and Releases.
   What exact software versions and releases do you plan to use? What are the acceptable situations at which one can deviate from that plan?
5. Technical Landscape.
   For Development, Testing, Staging and Production, how many applications do need to be linked? What number of servers is to be used? Where will these servers be located and how will they be connected?
6. Data Volume and Performance Expectation.
   What is the targeted minimum performance goal? What is the expected ideal performance? How frequently will transfers initiated? What data volume is to be transferred?

Functional Parameters.

7. Generic Process Flow.
Can you clearly walk through the project life-cycle, including the project trigger and authorization, preparation, planning, execution, monitoring and closing? Have you covered, at least generically, variations and scope change management, reporting requirements, and the integration to budgeting and cost control aspects?

8. Object-Level Mappings.
Following the above generic process flow, are you able to outline the tentative object-level mappings with their relationships between SAP and Primavera? Have you clearly covered the definition of a project, the related selection criteria, and all key objects?

9. Number of Schedules.
Will the Master Schedule be split into more detailed schedules in Primavera? Will the relationship between SAP objects and Primavera objects be 1:1? Where will be discrepancies?

10. Reporting Requirements.
What kind of reporting should be provided out of what application? Where will Earned Value calculations be performed, now or envisioned in the long term? What is the main purpose of the respective reports?

11. Data Conversion.
How will projects be addressed that have already started at the time the SAP-Primavera solution goes live? Will a Primavera data conversion or data consolidation effort be required? May changes in SAP or Primavera configuration require the dealing with different historic information? Can it be expected that all data corporate-wide will be in a comparative state?

Business and Implementation Parameters

12. Implementation Cost Estimate.
What is a rough cost estimate (+/- 40%) for the implementation? What are the key conditions and influencing factors specific to this business?

13. Implementation Time Estimate.
    What is a rough estimate (+/- 40%) for the duration of
    the implementation? What are the key conditions and
    influencing factors specific to this business?
14. Organizational Context.
    What other aspects of this business organization
    describe or affect the project scope?
15. Engagement Approach.
    Is a distinct engagement approach preferred over
    another one? What specific expectations for engaging
    suppliers need to be considered?

Technical Parameters

1. Integration Platform

**Should an integration platform be used or not? How is
it to be evaluated? What capabilities does it need to
have?**

While in theory one could develop some middleware
platform from scratch, this does not make sense at a time when
many such platforms are available. There would be too many
decisions to be made and too many capabilities to be
programmed. Therefore a proven and scalable platform should
be used if ever possible.

Such a platform will have EAI capabilities, be proven for the
integration between SAP and Primavera, with proven scalability
in respect to functionality (e.g. API extensions, alternative data
sources), access control, data integrity, and transfer logs. It
should also have the ability to support a number of potentially
changing technology standards (e.g. operating systems,
databases).

The above requirements should be the main criteria used to
explore its capabilities. Existing corporate infrastructure
standards should be leveraged if ever possible. This includes

such aspects like SAP NetWeaver, operating systems, SQL or Oracle databases.

> ***My Recommendation.*** Use an advanced but lightweight EAI platform that comes with pre-delivered SAP and Primavera adapters, a scalable and flexible mapping mechanism, support for various operating systems and databases, supported by a major corporation. My default recommendation is SAP-EPC, for the same reason spelled out in great detail below (Step 3).

2. Build vs. Buy

To what degree are solution components to be purchased? When should the decision be made to build them yourself?

There are only two situations in which it can make sense to yourself build a SAP-Primavera integration solution, or key enhancing components, and that is with the goal to:

(A) Either to turn the capabilities of the solution into part of your proprietary service offering yourself; or

(B) You are trying to integrate Primavera integration, or SAP integration plus Primavera integration into an independent product of yours.

In both situations this then becomes part of an attempt to gain a corporate competitive advantage through an offering on the market. I am aware of similar endeavors by large contractors. Larsen and Toubro Infotech started out that way with the precursor of what later turned into Primavera's Inspire product. Halliburton did something similar with regards to SAP-MS Project integration. And Ecosys claim to be able to have SAP integration and Primavera integration capabilities as part of their overall solution offering.

In 2000, I asked a small team of experts for the first time to develop a tool that integrates SAP and Primavera. Since then I have worked with half a dozen of different integration tools and approaches, several of which I helped design and build from ground up. The one common theme is that one can make rapid early progress linking SAP and Primavera quickly, and ugly, and with limited functionality, many breakpoints, little scalability, sparse practical usability, and not considering running it in real life. Yes, some data will be flowing, but that is about it.

Anything beyond that very soon turns into a difficult and drawn-out process, requiring lots of thinking, effort and time. As both somebody who offered products in this market and who has been providing services to deliver mature solutions for years on top of third party platforms, it has been one of the most difficult markets I have seen. Knowing what I do, if I were the CIO of a company I would take any help I can get, and risks from known knowns to unknown unknowns would be on the forefront of my mind.

It is easy to underestimate what it takes. When niche players invest man-years of focused efforts delivered by experienced teams, just to increase stability functions, enhanced API components, conditional updates capabilities, or advanced performance or error handling - buy and don't build. This statement does not just apply to the underlying platform, but to key enhancement aspects also. Yes, an experienced ABAP developer can add another field to a standard BAPI in SAP, but will she do so in a way that optimizes performance, allows for efficient back-end calls out of XSLT, and is easy to support in the context of an integration product like SAP-EPC?

On the other hand, it could be fun, couldn't it? For example, if there is no clear business case yet anyway but a big budget. Or your IT department has nothing else to do. Or if time is not of the essence and you are looking for a good way to train up a support unit that would hardly ever be needed if they just would have to work with a really mature product. Or if you happen to have technical people with a handful of different skills around that you would like to keep busy.

Yeah, why would you buy something proven if you could establish your own software development unit, train up people in a number of skills, lengthily analyze requirements, build prototypes, test and redesign, come up with a range of different and new scenarios, rebuild and retest, and eventually turn the focus into stabilizing the product at some point in time. Wouldn't it be more fun than just buying something mature and proven on the market and focus on your boring core business?

Continuing my sarcastic rant, re-inventing the wheel at a higher cost, higher risk and long delays can make sense - but only if you just try hard enough to come up with some reasons. They are of course not arguments that would earn you a raise or promotion in most organizations on the globe, but I never said I have all the answers, did I?

Hopefully you really did realize that with my last few statements I have been sarcastic here.

My Recommendation. Buy many solution aspects as possible rather than building them. This applies to the platform, but also to API extensions, functional components, performance optimization tools, error handling, and reporting and usability features. You are not in the business of developing IT products - unless you are, and then this is a totally different perspective.

3. Supportability

To what degree do you expect to support the solution in-house?

Keep in mind the complexity of the application, and the many moving parts that I keep referring to and that are defined in a complete technical landscape document. Reflect these complexities in the support approach also. Skills to support the various components should in principle be broadly available.

For example, if ABAP, Java, and XSLT are the core solution languages, sitting on standard web application servers like

WebLogic or NetWeaver, interacting with databases like SQL and Oracle, and the platform itself is supported by a major corporation, one already has a pretty good start. The solution should not use proprietary technologies that the average enterprise IT organization will not have special skills in. As long as comparably capable and reasonably priced solution components are available through an established supplier and on a common platform, those should be used.

The remaining question is then how to support the specific logic and process flow reflected in the solution as it is tailored for you. This is not quite as straightforward since it may be quite an investment, requiring knowledge of SAP and Primavera functionality, and of related technologies. The best approach then is to stress the need for sufficient logging and error handling capabilities that enable an internal team to identify and resolve issues themselves.

My Recommendation. The solution needs to be supportable internally and through straightforward and scalable support agreements and SLAs as much as possible. All platform and infrastructure aspects should be internally supported.

It should be possible to train the support team to identify issues and differentiate between those related to platform or infrastructure, to the APIs, to user errors, and finally to bugs of the specific solution implementation. However, do not attempt to build an internal SAP-Primavera development and support team, since almost all of the specific skills are likely to remain dormant for many months or years to come.

4. Software Versions and Releases

What exact software versions and releases do you plan to use? What are the acceptable situations at which one can deviate from that plan?

Most of the SAP-Primavera integration platforms on the market have been around for at least a handful of years, sometimes significantly longer (e.g. Impress). In theory they support a wide range of APIs and Primavera version or even releases of SAP ECC. As long as they use the SAP BAPI/RFC layer on the one side and the Primavera Java API on the other side, there is little in terms of releases that cannot in theory be supported.

Having all of that said, please don't inject "ancient" (= formally unsupported) releases into the mix. As long as it works, it works. But things can get very ugly very quickly. For example, some Primavera releases have data integrity issues that occur only in certain, and usually quite rare, situations. Those seem to be fixed in recent releases but not in old ones.

Now consider what would happen to the confidence level of a scheduler in Primavera if duplicate data showed up coming out of SAP. Think about the implication! You could not trust the schedule anymore, and it would always be in the back of your mind that the interface may have messed up your data. To add to that, the release would not be supported anymore and there is no good way to get help.

No, don't go down that road, and don't add artificially to complexity. Stay with reasonably recent versions and releases of the various software components that make up any integration solution. And keep in mind that data integrity issues like the one above may not be totally resolved even with new software releases, which is another reason to use proven and enhanced solution components.

My Recommendation. The releases of software used should be as recent as possible. Establish a policy that makes it next to impossible to use anything but the latest two supported releases on the market. This should apply particularly for Primavera P6 and the relating APIs, databases, or application servers (including NetWeaver).

5. Technical Landscape

For Development, Testing, Staging and Production, how many applications do need to be linked? What number of servers is to be used? Where will these servers be located and how will they be connected?

All mature solutions to integrate SAP and Primavera have a high level of similar landscape requirements. They all use the APIs on both sides (SAP BAPIs and Primavera Java API), have some sort of adapter, some middleware mapping tool usually built using Java, logging and data integrity and authorization and authentication tools, a few tools for administering the solution, and some user front-end to select data and initiate or schedule transfers.

In other words, we are not just talking about a little plug-in for Primavera or SAP. As this indicates there are common complexities, and mostly for good reasons. Indeed it is amazing to see the big picture similarities, which makes the differences in detailed approaches the more noticeable. But I would digress if I would already here start making my case for the use of SAP EPC. That will come later in my suggested Step 3.

Considering the above, to deliver great functionality and performance and to support business requirements, you should make a couple of early landscape design decisions.

First, decide on the number of applications to be linked. Will you use one SAP ECC production instance (typically the case) to link to one Primavera database shared across the enterprise? Or will you split the number of Primavera databases for support or regulatory reasons? The last question is not always straightforward to answer. Almost everybody aspires consolidation of Primavera instances, but that may not always be possible.

It is important to understand the chosen path early on, however, since there are implications. The technical design may need to change, even the user interface. The location of servers and related performance may be impacted, and parts of the implementation effort may be increased.

Second, decide on the numbers of logical servers to be used, and on their location. In general it is a good idea to put the Primavera API on a separate server from the Primavera database, and in the case of SAP EPC to use a separate server for NetWeaver, where the EPC Java component sits.

In case of a required split into separate Primavera database there are separate options for consolidating, or not, NetWeaver and API servers. It may be advisable to use a separate NetWeaver installation per Primavera API and Primavera database over a consolidation of NetWeaver and Primavera API even in the case of multiple Primavera database installations.

Important decision-making criteria involve security, code interdependencies, supportability, and performance. This is one of the situations where some analysis of the overall solution adds significant value, and external advice from experienced personnel should be sought if ever possible.

> *My Recommendation.* Always try to keep the solution as simple as possible. Aim for the use of one SAP ECC environment and one Primavera database environment (including API server) located at one geographical location and on the same LAN. Then go from there by allowing exceptions if business reasons warrant so.
>
> Keep in mind that a logical separation of servers adds complexity and geographical separation adds to performance challenges. If you intend to move from the 1:1 localized solution, analyze carefully and seek external advice.

6. Data Volume and Performance Expectations

What is the targeted minimum performance goal? What is the expected ideal performance? How frequently will transfers initiated? What data volume is to be transferred?

Sometimes I hear statements like "when I save it in Primavera it should be in SAP". As mentioned below, in Pitfall #1, this is neither a technically realistic path, nor should it be desired functionality. What is important is to early on get a good general understanding of the data volumes and frequency of transfers required. These pieces of information can impact the technical and functional solution architecture, and the implementation approach.

Let's be clear, however, that at this point in the process we need to differentiate between requirements and expectations. The frequency of transfers and the ability to transfer a certain data volume in principle are requirements. The expected throughput and time to align a certain data volume are expectations.

For example, if turnarounds required updates four times a day, and each time 40,000 activities would need to be transferred, and each transfer would take 8 hours - we would have a problem. This would be even aggravated if three turnarounds would be going on at the same time, using the same Primavera API and the same instance of the integration product.

The requirements then can be expressed this way: "The solution needs to be able to support the synchronization of up to three simultaneous transfer four times a day, aligning data between up to 40,000 activities each."

Now I do not want to generate the impression that three times 40,000 activities, or 120,000 in total, could in all cases reasonably be expected to be transferred within an hour or two. They may not need to either, since there are other ways of increasing performance. Such ways may not just affect the technical landscape but also the functional solution design and transfer logic.

It also helps evaluating how long it takes for a Primavera client to open a large project. It may take five minutes to open a 15,000 activities project. Should that be the case, as I have seen myself, don't expect that transferring the same number of activities, applying logic, and going through the SAP and Primavera APIs would be as fast or faster than a "simple" pull of that data by a thick client.

> **My Recommendation.** Identify the data volume and required frequency of transfers. Consider the volume of individual projects, and of an expected number of related projects that may be triggered at the same time. Translate that into a set of minimum requirements, and consider them when designing your technical solution landscape and when defining expectations relating to functional mappings and related logic.

Functional Parameters

7. Generic Process Flow

Can you clearly walk through the project life cycle? Have you covered, at least generically, variations and scope change management, reporting requirements, and the integration to budgeting and cost control aspects?

Describe the generic process flow, including the project trigger and authorization, followed by the preparation, planning, execution, monitoring and closing phases. Make clear that the process in almost all conceivable situations starts in SAP on some level, although from that point on there can be big variations.

Look at the process not just as a series of object level mappings (e.g. "in SAP a high-level WBS structure is created reflecting a CBS, then transferred into Primavera where it is expanded into lower-level structures"). Go beyond a pure look at structures, and consider aspects of cost (budget, forecast, actuals), time, resources, and progress. Also describe how changes in scope will be managed and by whom.

The goal of this exercise is to move beyond a static mapping view, and contemplate some of the key elements of the dynamic elements of the integration, going beyond the pure logical interaction of data elements. For example, should a status change be controlled by Primavera, or will a date on a procurement document in SAP provide meaningful input to a scheduler in Primavera, or will a certain step to run a report or filter in Primavera require cost reference data to be transferred from SAP?

My Recommendation. Describe a complete typical project life cycle by walking through it multiple times, covering various perspectives like status, structures, cost, and time. Do not try to cover all details, but familiarize yourself with some of the more obvious consequences of general life-cycle decisions about these topics.

8. Object-Level Mappings

Following the above generic process flow, are you able to outline the tentative object-level mappings with their relationships between SAP and Primavera? Have you clearly covered the definition of a project, the related selection criteria, and all key objects?

Describe the tentative object-level mappings, e.g. the relationships between objects in SAP and in Primavera, including their rationale. It should be specified whether there is a 1:1 relationship between project structures in SAP and in Primavera, or whether Primavera goes more into detail. For example, should SAP work orders become Primavera WBS Elements only, WBS Summary Activities, or only show up as fields on task-dependent activities?

As a general starting point, try to leave the basic responsibility for the following objects with the application as I list it here. This keeps them in line with generally accepted strengths of each application.

- SAP.
  High level project structures (at least), budget

(approved money), cost (actuals), cash flow, resources (but not necessarily resource assignments), actual hours
• Primavera.
Detailed scope (if not provided by SAP), relationships, schedule, percent completion progress

Also try to stay as "straightforward" as possible. Apply some degree of Occam's Razor, paraphrased as selecting the mapping that requires the lowest number of logical transformations and assumptions.

As objects, consider Projects, WBS, activities, labor and non-labor resources, resource assignments, relationships, dates, progress, and cost, in both applications. Keep in mind that mappings may not be 1:1. I have seen clients deriving a Primavera project based on selections of a SAP Project, a SAP WBS Element, a Revision, or a combination of various factors.

The goal of this exercise is not to be complete, but to think through key decisions, mainly on the highest level of how to derive the scope of work to be transferred. If nothing more is achieved, this allows for an educated guess and a more realistic demonstration and reference of a generic process, as the actual implementation starts. For example, the first four digits of a Functional Location in conjunction with a Project ID could be the main selection criteria and mapping for what is considered a Primavera project and related scope. If so, then a demonstration and scope and design review should use a similar set of criteria during the demonstration, and not a selection based on revision codes.

My Recommendations. Map out the object-level mappings, starting out with having each application "owning" objects relating to its natural strength, and an attempt to keep logical transformations of mappings as simple as possible.

9. Number of Schedules

Will the Master Schedule be split into more detailed schedules in Primavera? Will the relationship between SAP objects and Primavera objects be 1:1? Where will be discrepancies?

The most straightforward mapping matches objects between SAP and Primavera on a one-to-one basis. The SAP project relates to exactly one Primavera project, the WBS structure is exactly replicated in both environments, the numbers of activities (or sometimes operations in SAP PM terms) are the same in both applications, as are the resource libraries and resource assignments. Changes in the structure of one environment will exactly be replicated in the other one.

In the context of a turnaround this aspect of the solution usually works by-and-large like that, or close enough to that example, and it usually does so well. It is more rarely the case in the world of capital projects, whether from the owner's perspective or from the general contractor's perspective, or for complex engineering and design or sales-driven complex make-to-order projects.

In the latter cases, one finds two kinds of complicating factors, both of which may need to be considered in concert.

The first one is that the project-level mapping still is 1:1, but that the project in Primavera may go to a lower level of detail than the one in SAP. In Primavera you may take a WBS from SAP, often reflecting a high-level finance-driven Cost Breakdown Structure (CBS), and break it down into lower level WBS structures that are only needed to facilitate schedule development and management. SAP activities may purely relate to Primavera summary activities, which implies that additional logic calculations need to be performed during transfers.

The second and even higher-impact factor is when you break out a Master Schedule into lower-level schedules, reflected as separate Primavera projects, and the integrated solution is to support the complete process flow. This may severely enhance the scope of the implementation, while also adding significant additional value.

Clarifying the general design in respect to the above structural factors aids in assessing implementation challenges and implementation approaches. For example, it may introduce the need for more elaborate blueprinting efforts, make prototypes even more indispensable during the detailed design phase, and lead to more complex and lengthy test cases and scenarios.

My Recommendations. Building on the generic process flow and the object-level mappings, define where 1:1 relationships between SAP and Primavera project structures will not be sufficient anymore. Identify whether this is purely a matter of keeping more details in Primavera as compared to SAP, or whether it assumes the replicating or breaking out of a Primavera project into duplicate or sub-components.

10. Reporting Requirements

What kind of reporting should be provided out of what application? Where will Earned Value calculations be performed, now or envisioned in the long term? What is the main purpose of the respective reports?

Consider this (real) conversation that I witnessed a few weeks ago:

Prospective Client:	"Are you live with this solution."
Consultant:	"Yes, we are live and it is used in production."
Prospective Client:	"What kind of reports do you get out of Primavera?"
Consultant:	"Beyond the standard ones pre-delivered by Primavera?"
Prospective Client:	"Yes."

Consultant: "Well, none yet. We are still working on this. It is being addressed in the next release."

In the above situation the implementation of the solution even involved the implementation of a business analytics engine for advanced cross-application reporting. But the business was not been ready for it yet.

This is not an unusual situation. It is not necessarily even a bad one. Reporting is not the only benefit one gets out of an integrated solution. It may not even be one of the main benefits and there may be reasons to live with new layouts and standard reports in Primavera or SAP.

What is important early on, though, is to describe in general the expectations for reporting and its targeted implementation time. A SAP-Primavera integration solution should support the reporting of KPIs for project reviews and stage gates. It should also lay the foundation to introduce earned value reporting, or at least "earned value-type reporting".

The most basic decision to be taken early on is then about what kind of reports are envisioned out of each application. For example, you may want to use Primavera as a reporting tool to submit project status reports to your clients, or want to use it for earned value and progress reports to evaluate contractor schedules. In that case, make sure that expectations about data mappings reflect this requirement. Alternatively, the requirements are different if you intend to keep earned value reports in SAP for tighter integration into SAP PPM, or use an external reporting engine.

As a side comment, this kind of reporting is not to be confused with reports about the data transfers themselves. Such reports may become audit tools, or function as simulations of transfers or to support the analysis of data transfer or even data consistency issues. They are not business reports per se, though, and fall into the realm of end-user features and support.

My Recommendation. Be upfront about the general reporting vision, and what reports are to be supported in principle in SAP PS or PM, Primavera, the portfolio management product (e.g. SAP PPM), or through an analytics or intelligence tool like Cognos, Business Objects, or Hyperion. Among others, consider cost reports, progress reports, earned value reports, and general key performance indictors to be supported by the SAP-Primavera integration solution.

11. Data Conversion

How will projects be addressed that have already started at the time the SAP-Primavera solution goes live? Will a Primavera data conversion or data consolidation effort be required? May changes in SAP or Primavera configuration require the dealing with different historic information? Can it be expected that all data corporate-wide will be in a similarly state of quality?

Let's first consider an ideal scenario: Most integration processes I have seen start out with a brave new world where a project gets initiated through a sales order or a portfolio decision. A high-level structure gets established in SAP and budgets get assigned, and then data is transferred into Primavera and the project plan is gradually expanded. This is "clean" and controlled.

It is not always realistic, though. What happens then when long-term projects have been going on and need to be integrated into a newly established integrated SAP-Primavera solution?

The short answer here is that this has a serious potential to get "messy". At that point the interface is unable to map project structures and objects between the two applications. For example, without manual intervention the system cannot know which Primavera activity relates to which SAP activity. This relationship then needs to be established manually.

As with all manual processes, this is error-prone. Here, your transfer tools can provide some relief, if you consider these additional requirements early on. Specific transfer reports and the additional interpretation of errors can become a powerful tool to support data conversion activities. You should know early on whether this is required, though. For the fixing of issues, mappings are to allow manual corrections of IDs, and this will change and add to the underlying mapping approach.

Additionally the interface may need to make a decision about which data fields may be owned by which application at the more advanced stage in its life cycle that a specific project is at. The resulting solution goes beyond automated mappings of IDs between applications.

The overall implication is therefore not only an effort for the cleansing of data, and the need for manual interference to add SAP keys into Primavera. While data conversion activities can be facilitated and simplified through a powerful interface, this also adds a number of additional design requirements that should be addressed at the very beginning of the integration project.

Finally, data conversion activities and their relation to cutover and Go Live efforts may also require running parallel Primavera environments until old projects are phased out. This may be needed particularly if multiple Primavera environments are to be consolidated, or if the integration into SAP may trigger a substantial re-configuration of Primavera.

When clarifying this parameter, you do not need to resolve and address all the above implications. Just clarify to what degree data conversion is in scope or not, so that the implications can be considered during more advanced and specific design activities.

> ***My Recommendation.*** Exclude data conversion activities wherever possible. Should that not be a reasonable option, be upfront about it and include this into the early functional and technical design of the solution. Keep in mind that at this invariably will add additional effort, risks, and costs to the project.

Business Parameters

12. Implementation Cost Estimate

What is a rough cost estimate (+/- 40%) for the implementation? What are the key conditions and influencing factors specific to this business?

Imagine you would want to buy a new computer. You go to the Apple store and look at all the wonderful devices. After a long evaluation you finally decide to go with this great, state-of-the-art MacBook Pro. Since Apple is upfront about it you have considered the price dimension from the get go.

Now imagine a different situation and that there were no prices communicated upfront. Apple would not tell you what it costs until after you made a decision. Then they drop the $2,750 price bomb for the top-of-the-line laptop, with some caveats that it could easily be more if you wanted to buy all the other recommended equipment also (like a power cable).

Sometimes I feel like the second example when I notice how service organizations negotiate. Maybe I am just not a sales guy, and maybe I am not the smartest negotiator around. Both are certainly true. But I do believe in the value of quality and low risk and good performance.

Therefore I do like to make some general parameters clear from the outset. The budget for external implementation services to deliver a solution to a large enterprise is likely to end up between $250,000 and $500,000. This is probably matched by a similar number for software and additional tools that limit risk and address typical enhancements (like performance optimization, conditional updates, etc.), hardware and internal labor. If you assume these dimensions, you are probably in the right ballpark.

There are exceptions and I have been involved in much more expensive and some lower-priced implementations. As a rule of thumb, though, these numbers work. They can also be validated by applying specialist rates for the two to three resources that on average are involved (covering functional support, installation, technical), and multiplying it by the duration of a typical implementation in an enterprise context (see the next parameter).

My Recommendation. Assume a budget between $250,000 and $500,000 for implementation services, plus charges for the integration platforms and potential additional prefabricated tools and capabilities. This assumes "middle-of-the-road" answers for most of the other parameters, like an exclusion of rollouts, a straightforward system landscape, no multi-level schedules, a by-and-large typical number of custom requirements, and an organization that is not too complex.

The scope itself usually affects the cost only by about 20% to 25%. The organizational complexity or the specific logistical context of an integration project, like it being part of a new SAP or Primavera rollout, could have a bigger impact than that. Data conversion requirements move the costs more toward the higher end, as do expectations to optimize performance, or elaborate testing requirements.

13. Implementation Time Estimate

What is a rough estimate (+/- 40%) for the duration of the implementation? What are the key conditions and influencing factors specific to this business?

Obviously SAP-Primavera integration needs to be implemented before the end of the year... It always has to, at least initially, and is independent of where you are in the year, until November. Then is moved to "Q I next year" which then becomes "end of the year" again a few months later. That is how it so often seems to work, but sometimes the calendar year does not seem to matter that much and the question becomes more one of bottom-up estimation.

I also have a rule of thumb for this one. To answer this question, I will start with asking one myself: How often have you seen an enterprise organization deliver any business solution in less than three months? And what if it was a complex solution with many technical components and multiple business applications? And what if SAP and Oracle were involved? And what if this was about impacting the ability of the whole corporation to execute on critical business strategies?

The lower limit is set by complexity, of the organization, the applications involved, the business processes, the technologies, and the ability of the organization to digest all of this. Communication, internal processes, the need for alignment and risk reduction, the need to properly test - consider all these factors properly. Do no try to rush these beyond an organization's ability to understand, accept, adapt, and adopt. Buy-in is too important to justify the taking of shortcuts.

So there - finally - comes my rule of thumb: Hardly ever anything gets done faster than within three months, while equally rarely there is a need to go far beyond six months. This is when a competent team is involved, using a proven toolset. To be on the safe side I add a small margin and call it 4 to 8 months. But it is also almost totally independent of scope!

The general building blocks for these 4 to 8 months are as follows. Assume:

- A formal scope validation phase takes a couple of weeks, including related documentation and sign-off.
- A formal blueprint phase takes about 4 to 8 weeks, including one or two sets of workshops, detailed documentation, test script definition, a prototype mocking up the specifications, and the preparation of environments.
- The formal building and unit testing of the solution takes about 4 to 8 weeks also, and includes the setting up of test environments.
- Assume three integration test cycles of one to two weeks each, plus two or three user acceptance test cycles of one to two weeks also.
- The cutover preparation takes another couple of weeks. From that point on you are in post-Go Live support.

These durations could be longer if they are coupled with a new SAP implementation or are part of a serious upgrade of SAP or significant process standardization or change management efforts. They may be shorter in smaller organizations, particularly if they have less corporate standards in place that govern decisions and their implementation.

My Recommendation. Assume that a typical implementation will take between 4 and 8 months. Try to be realistic about where your organization is, and consider the other technical and functional parameters. Rarely will it be faster, rarely will it be longer, almost totally independent of scope! But - to achieve that, be prepared to have a good project manager involved who is able to get the various departments and suppliers in line.

14. Organizational Scope

What other aspects of this business organization describe or affect the project scope?

Some obvious organizational context has an impact on the project scope. The industry and the process to be addressed are prime examples. It does of course make a substantial difference whether one implements an SAP-Primavera integration to address the management of turnarounds at an oil refinery, or to improve the way an engineering and construction (ENC) company constructs a skyscraper, or an engineering firm builds a nuclear power plant.

Other more detailed questions help answering the more general one from above:

- Is this part of a multi-stage implementation? Will this be a Pilot only, to be rolled out only after a post-Go Live evaluation? What are the plans or expectations for rolling out the solution across the enterprise?
- What short-term drivers affect the targeted project schedule, like an upcoming outage, or a contractually obligated delivery of a complex product?
- Would you see value in a Proof-of-Concept (POC) that helps clarify project scope for the internal project team?
- How prepared is the organization? Is this solution combined with a process standardization effort, possibly involving configuration changes in SAP or in Primavera?
- How many independent business units will be targeted with the solution? Are processes aligned across those? Are they all sufficiently represented? What will be done if they are not?
- Is the SAP-Primavera integration project part of a bigger endeavor, like the implementation of SAP or of Primavera, or a substantial upgrade of asset management capabilities?

It really helps being upfront about this. I sometimes see two extremes, both of which should be prevented. On the one hand organizations or people in organizations are overly confident about where they are. Beware of that and respect the challenge. On the other hand people downplay their maturity and what they can achieve. They use the "crawl - walk - run" metaphor to lower expectations, in my opinion misjudging and underestimating the opportunity they have to achieve substantially improved solutions.

My Recommendation. Consider all detailed questions listed above and provide a realistic assessment of the organizational project context. Review to what degree that tangibly will affect the project approach, charter, or plan. Definitely share it with the external service providers you may engage to get their realistic feedback - as soon as possible so that there are no negative surprises.

15. Engagement Approach

Is a distinct engagement approach preferred over another one? What specific expectations for engaging suppliers need to be considered?

Some of the most successful SAP-Primavera solution implementations I have been involved in were directly managed by a committed project manager from the client, staying on top of a project plan and statement of work, and clearing the path by keeping all suppliers and contractors in line and focused on the plan. Whenever required, the technical experts delivering the integration functionality were able to directly interact with the client and with the onsite consultants supporting processes.

To prevent having to hire an unnecessarily large number of skilled resources for an extended period of time, be prepared to assume that a big chunk of the project work will be done offsite. This will drive down the overall solution cost, and increase quality and reduce risk. While these benefits are usually too big to disregard, this works best when two onsite functions are clearly addressed: a project manager and a business liaison. These functions may be performed by the same person, by two people, or at times through a Systems Integrator (SI) by a group of people.

To achieve the involvement of specialized skills whenever necessary and wherever possible, a fixed price approach is more flexible than a time and expense (T&E) approach, at least for the centerpiece of the project.

One proven option is to perform most of the delivery as a fixe price, and then move toward a time and expense based engagement for rollout or support, or even earlier during advanced test cycles. SAP-Primavera projects don't lend themselves to time and material-based engagements. The complexity of the work requires too many different skills, tools to be used, and external systems contributing to the project.

It is then not economical to hire, let's say, five people for a long period of time, particularly when project duration is not totally locked down. It neither is effective to hire individuals just because they have a certain skill set. It is the team that makes things happen, and the understanding and experience of how various pieces of work relate to each other.

I have had inconsistent experiences using System Integrators. There can be frictions if motivations are not completely aligned. Often SIs work on a T&E basis, while the other implementers work for a fixed price. Sometimes they try to bully the real experts, or to use them simply to open the door to new business. A lack of alignment almost brought a big project in Sydney, Australia, to its knees. The only way to rescue it was to play along with the T&E contractors, put solution delivery above money, take the losses and roll with the wave.

This is not sustainable of course, and should be avoided at any cost.

Such issues are less accentuated but still present when multiple suppliers perform supporting IT functions. In the 2010s this is almost always the case. General support is outsourced, hardware setup is outsourced, and a number of contractors support various functional or development tasks. Again the solution is good project management. Formality can be uncomfortable, but more often than not it has proven to be helpful.

My Recommendation. While there is a great variation of engagement approaches that can work, in general I recommend to have the core solution delivered at a fixed price by a team that has proved that it can deliver SAP-Primavera integration. The client should perform the project management role.

Link milestones and related payments to clearly specified deliverables, and clarify the logistics of contractual aspects with all vendors upfront. Keep the project plan flexible without allowing substantial performance variations where dependencies affect other team members.

3.

HOW? PICK THE RIGHT TOOLS

Software Vendor Selection

The process of selecting technical integration tools often makes me wonder...

Over the last 15 years I must have been involved, in one way or another, in many dozens vendor and tool selection processes. Companies want to see presentations, have technical questions, implementation questions, process questions, sometimes formal RFIs and RFPs or RFQs. Sometimes they look at SAP-Primavera integration as part of the selection of an ERP product and sometimes as part of the evaluation of Primavera as a project management or scheduling tool.

The Approach is 'Off'.

One common theme of most of these vendor selection processes is that they are very much technocratic on the one side, and mapping focused on the other side. The evaluators usually seem to assume that they do know real and specific requirements and would already have identified which real solutions address these requirements. With such a context it then seems logical to indeed just verify whether an integration platform is capable of delivering a very specific capability in a very specific way.

In many cases, though, the real requirement may have been misinterpreted, the real solution may just be one option of many, and not the most effective or likely one. And above all, "in principle" any halfway serious EAI platform can deliver almost anything.

The real question is how.

Since one cannot really identify and design solutions during a procurement process, of course I ask myself often whether this is for real or whether it is just another case of a Milking Cow (see above).

Even though usually business people are involved also, the focus often is on what really are technical matters. The most frequent type of question is "Can it do this?", followed by "Can you show me?" While I appreciate such concerns, even with respect to such aspects the questions are somewhat "off". They don't address some of the most critical aspects, while putting an almost impossible hurdle in front of any decision.

The Missing Requirements.

First let's review the missing critical aspects. Almost all selection processes try to assess the technical capabilities of a product by asking about its ability to reflect specific functional requirements.

Come again?

Let me describe it this way: To evaluate whether a product is capable, typical questions involve specific mappings, specific logical conditions, and specific fields. That is like exploring the value of a car not by asking whether it drives, but wanting to see in real life whether it can drive from Boise to Salt Lake City, and from LA to San Diego, and from Boston to Augusta.

It is a car. It drives. This is how it drives. See it drive. And now believe that it will drive where you are pointing it at.

Likewise the software just needs to work. The solution needs to deliver **whatever** the business requests, as long as it is within some fairly general reasonable parameters.

My standard answer is that in principle everything is possible that can be described logically consistently. That is almost it. Yes, a live demo is helpful and should be part of the evaluation. But those are easy to come by. Yes, a talk with reference clients can be helpful, although one needs to be aware that their processes and implementation context likely have been substantially different from yours. And yes, a quick look under the hood can be revealing also.

This still leaves out some of the key questions, though. In the example of the car, what is the gas mileage, what is its loading or towing capabilities, how long does it last, what are the warranties, and so on. Here the analogies start breaking down somewhat, but not totally yet.

In respect to a SAP-Primavera integration tool, some comparable and more technical questions should be:

- What about performance?
- What about logs and custom error handling?
- What about extendibility?
- What about support for technical standards?
- What about simulations?
- What about data integrity?
- How would one go about redesigning a complete process?
- How is configuration and customization done in principle?
- How does one support the application?
- What architectural requirements and what skills are required to use the tool(s)?

The Impossible Hurdle.

There is also the impossible hurdle that is being raised. Twice in the past few months the following happened to me: A business provides me with a list of questions about the ability of EPC. I demonstrate, live, EPC capabilities relating to almost each individual aspect being questioned about, often pointing out several options of addressing the underlying business question. Anything not demonstrated live I address in detail through specific explanations.

The next thing I hear the business wants to do a "Proof of Concept" using a very specific process flow. They do not really want answers to in-principle questions. They are not satisfied in seeing basic capabilities.

They want to see their specific solution reflected in a very specific demonstration. If you need to do a more realistic POC to help narrowing down scope, by all means go ahead. Just don't see it as part of the vendor or tool selection!

It is part of an implementation. Totally justified and usually a very reasonable step. But because it is part of the implementation, make the tool selection upfront and use the full set of tools that you ultimately need anyway to get the job done.

Don't assume you should start with a clean slate of sample mappings and would get very far. Turn it into a mini-project, use the full set of tools and not just the platform and generic installation. Don't do a POC asking how one could start from scratch using the generic template. Why do it the hard way, limiting the relevancy of what you are trying to prove?

The 'Fake POC' Installation.

A favorite theme in this context is what I call the "Fake POC" installation. To explore the capabilities of a platform, a business installs the platform. Naturally they then want to start playing around with it, just to realize that just hacking away is not going to be a satisfactory experience.

It is like buying a Spanish CD to proof that one really can express complex thoughts in Spanish. Don't you have to learn it first? Don't you have to have a plan, a project? Or to stay in the above picture, if you want to test-drive a car, do you really need to test-drive all its possible uses, with the same number of passengers, variations of loads, and specific commutes between specific locations?

The result has to be that either (a) one is dissatisfied with the "out-of-the-box" handling of the tool because it seems so far off what I want to see as the end product, or (b) one adjusts the evaluation process by acknowledging that "in principle" the tool has proven itself although nothing coherent could be seen. There probably is some sort of (c) out there also, but then this exercise does not make much sense to me in the first place.

Do you really wonder whether a product that you have seen working live in several ways, and that has been implemented at a number of client, could be installed?

Or do you really wonder whether you could re-create complex processes (of course called "simple") by doing not much more than playing around with some code and capabilities? Aided by a "consultant"?

So not even seeing is believing anymore?

Or are you out for a "real POC" by somebody giving you a working prototype of the solution you want as part of a platform selection process? There I see the cow again...

How to better go about it.

So how should one go about selecting tools? This question is simpler than it sounds. Follow the three steps outlined on the following pages and you will do fine. Before you do so, make sure you are clear about the strategic parameters described above. Then follow this guideline, and you will select the right tool.

Then it is off to design the right solution and implementing it.

3 Considerations for Tools Selection

Selecting the right tools requires three steps:

(1) Decide to Buy.

Should you not want to buy the tools, the selection process is over. In most cases this is a fake argument, though. This question is almost settled as much as whether mankind can travel to the moon. Sure, there are doubters out there, but almost none of us spends much time agonizing about that topic anymore.

My recommendation here is not surprising and very simple: Buy. You are not in the business of building software, are you (unless you are, of course)? You don't want to be dependent on an individual developer, do you? You want to stay flexible to support changing platforms, don't you? You want a solution sooner rather than later, don't you? (See Myth 6, below).

It does not end with picking the integration platform itself, though. The picture is a bit larger.

(2) Compare generic platform options and capabilities.

Use a quick checklist to verify that you are considering a real and capable platform, e.g. mapping orchestration, multi-threading, batching, splitting up into multiple databases, authorization controls, ensuring data integrity, adapter to SAP, adapter to Primavera, error handling and management, ability to connect to additional data sources and potentially other applications, and support for various operating systems and databases.

Make sure the tool is lightweight enough and capable enough to not fall over when hardware changes, other software applications are picked, or releases change.

Essentially this means that you need a mature enterprise application integration platform. In theory it could be almost any EAI platform, although we are talking about a specialized market here. Below I will go in more detail about the usual suspects.

(3) Identify additional tool requirements and their availability.

This is where things get even more interesting. Generic EAI platform capabilities are one thing; the ability to deliver robust solution components quickly and in a proven manner is another one. Examples are already existing pre-built extensions of the APIs, performance-optimizing features, user-friendly features, functionality enhancing components, and advanced templates.

Once the above steps have been followed, you should be able to make a decision quickly and move on.

(1) Confirm the Basic Approach: Decide to Buy

In "Guns, Germs, and Steel" Pulitzer-prize winning author Jared Diamond describes that throughout all of human history the concept of writing was invented at most five times, and possibly even less often. What does that mean - that humans in general are too lazy (or too efficient?) to keep reinventing the wheel (or writing)?

Translating that into the realm of technology, are we really surprised how rarely people re-invent the TV or the computer or the phone? Apart from Apple, I mean. I guess we are not really surprised, but I am still amazed by how often business and IT teams of large organizations seem to have a different attitude when it comes to other technical solutions.

Let's just say you wanted to integrate two complex software applications, when lots of components for frequently encountered integration challenges are readily available. Do you really prefer to go through the whole trial-and-error or analysis-and-design or ramp-up-the-learning-curve effort again, instead of buying what is readily available?

The first question to answer is whether you want to build an "interface" or the integration from ground up, or whether you want to buy it. I call this "confirm" the basic approach to buy, because hopefully you have set this as one of your strategic parameters at the outset of your pre-project work. The decision to buy instead of build should have been made.

The reason why I still keep mentioning it as a first step is because during the selection process of tools there is a tendency of questioning over and over again the value of using specific platforms or pre-build components, advanced add-ons, or enhancements that improve the robustness and capabilities of the generic solution.

Of course the IT department of almost any large organization would be capable of building many things from scratch. In almost all cases, though, this does not make sense. The technology world is too complex and costs, time, risk and quality would seriously be at stake.

This is more than just about the platform, but about the whole integration solution. Don't try to agonize over how much money you theoretically could save by re-inventing the wheel and building the little pieces that make up a robust or industrial-strength solution.

It is a typical challenge with complexity: The individual pieces are all not very difficult, but there are lots of little pieces and lots of moving parts. You may be a month or two in the process before you realize all the various skills required, the obstacles to be mastered, how many unknown questions have turned into known ones, wondering how many others are still out there.

Let's assume you are using SAP EPC. Sure, you can figure out generic mappings yourself as long as you have XSLT-skilled people. It may be more difficult when you need to start extending the API, e.g. by adding more fields to BAPIs. Then you will want to integrate those into the existing XSLT, just to realize that the sequence of steps of the template you use needs to be changed. Then you come up with a different workflow, realize that you need to find a way to support conditional updates, performance, documentation of the work, and the saga continues.

Before long you are deep in the thicket, spending ever more time analyzing and evaluating and thinking through options. That is when you realize that the principle of coding is not the real issue. It is how to code, what to code, how to fit the various pieces of code together, test them, document them, support them. You are likely to discover how difficult it can be to ask the right questions. ABAP coders are not XSL or Java programmers, Java or XSL programmers are not process experts, process experts are not SAP experts, SAP experts are not Primavera experts, Primavera experts may not understand specifics of the P6 Java API, Java API experts are unlikely to know all there is about SAP Basis or NetWeaver or other application servers. And these are just the skills.

Now coordinate that whole effort, explore the options, come up with an optimized system and solution landscape, and tell me how you think you can save money, reduce risk, be more efficient or even improve on the overall quality of the solution, as compared to using an out-of-the-box platform and related proven solution components.

My short answer is that it is nothing less than unrealistic. Decide to buy, as much as possible, and get over it. Don't fret the little things. Focus on the significant cost savings that are at stake, or even more the dramatic business value that can be generated in the long term. Time is money. Risk reduction is key. Quality is crucial. And overall costs will be lower also.

(2) Assess the Platform Options and Capabilities

SAP EPC

I can make it very easy for you. Here is my default and recommended pick for an integration platform.

Why It Is The Best. Go with a product proven on the market, mature, supported by one of the biggest software vendors on Earth, supporting all kinds of operating systems and databases. With NetWeaver, this product uses the same technology base that you have in house already, its transactions are triggered in the SAP User Interface, its authorizations are managed in the SAP ECC Basis System, transfer logs are accessible on the SAP ECC server, and its SAP Adapter is naturally powerful and supported natively.

Beyond this, EPC has an unsurpassed scalable mapping and logic, or "process orchestration" engine. It is expandable, and as an inherent EAI platform can be used to extend into third party databases or other project management applications.

EPC comes with a large number of out-of-the-box sample mappings that exemplify what the product can do. Its true strength, though, comes in when using the XSLT-based engine and using its easy-to-manipulate code to extend or customize workflows and logical steps, or when plugging in extensions and powerful add-ons and enhancements.

EPC 2.0 supports multi-threading, batching and links to multiple Primavera environments. It can be extended to deal with custom fields, custom BAPIs and RFCs, custom transactions, and even third party applications. We have used it as a Primavera-to-Primavera interface, made external database calls, and added functional extensions and features. All of that is seamlessly running on a Java-based platform, and the abilities to orchestrate a tailored process flow are almost limitless.

In short, the platform offers anything one needs, and a few extras one may want, from a scalable integration platform, in a still relatively lightweight package.

Some Context. EPC is not a native SAP product but the result of an acquisition. When that happened, around 2007, I had just sold a competing product myself, so knew the EPC team as well-respected competitors. The product originally was built by a company called LaborLogix, later renamed SOA Logix. After the acquisition, SAP Labs became the owner of the product.

Despite all the raving above I can prove that I am not just an SAP-fanboy. Let's look at some of the critical points, before returning to why the strengths supersede all those, and to why in summary the product beats anybody else in the overall score.

A Challenged Beginning. The product has come a long way, and truly deserves its status as the market leader. I would not have called it that before the first few implementations (or maybe even after them), and necessary upgrades to the platform.

It also helped that by now there have been a wide range of implementations that helped mature the product and creating a little ecosystem of add-ons, enhancements, and advanced features. These turn implementations nowadays into low-risk exercises. When done right, of course.

With my team from Competitive Edge International (CEI) I did the worldwide first two or three EPC implementations after the acquisition from SOA Logix. The beginning was intuitive at some times, ugly at others. The product was by far not as mature as it could have been. Installations were poorly documented and full of bugs. The functional capabilities were limited to standard SAP BAPIs, conditional updates were not available, WBS IDs could not fully be mapped, and error handling and related logging was not up to par.

Still it could be done, and the reason was - the great flexibility and scalability of the platform. Already then this was where EPC excelled. The XSLT and the extendibility to perform custom API calls give the system unsurpassed capabilities. And it addressed all of the urgent issues of the first few implementations. Now, more than five years after the acquisition, EPC 2.0 has significantly matured and the platform is second to none. SAP really came through with that.

Limitations. That does not mean that the out-of-the-box product is perfect. Particularly some of its default behavior has a narrow focus. EPC overwrites data every single time, offers good logs but doesn't cater to the end-user much, and has a few other idiosyncrasies that can make un-tuned implementations work a bit roughly.

Such shortcomings don't matter for in-principle demonstrations, or for narrow POCs. After that, the platform is what counts, and nothing else. As I will keep mentioning over and over again, implementations of the integration of SAP and Oracle are not installations (see below: Myth 1), so that is all good.

The Trouble with Marketing. The biggest beef I have with EPC is its initial positioning as a ready-to-use out-of-the-box product, focusing attention on sample mappings as if those could address in any way the requirements of any industrial-strength implementation. Indeed, the sample mappings do little more than show some of the basic and underlying capabilities.

In and of themselves they are quite limited. And they have to. How could SAP, or anybody else for that matter, pre-build solutions, let alone one single template, that address all variations of process flow and mappings and business processes for all industries and types of projects following all project management methodologies and considering any kind of configuration differences in SAP ECC or Primavera?! It is simply impossible.

An Expert's Perspective: How EPC won me over!

"I have to admit that my initial response to EPC was skeptical. Yet another suit of clothes on the old emperor. We were engaged in a fairly challenging project in Sydney and I was there to lead the ABAP team. I was aghast that the integration would be done in no less than three technologies: ABAP, XSLT and Java. The Java guys were excited and had big plans.

We decided to do it as much by the book as we could. There really wasn't much need for Java, as EPC provides a very comprehensive wrapper for the Primavera APIs. ABAP was a must: as is usual in SAP interfacing one just cannot get all the required information out of standard BAPIs. Our team had some XSLT experience from previous assignments and we ended holding this baby. The heart of EPC is an XSLT processing engine called Datapath. The power of the Datapath Engine combined with XLST was a revelation to me and I have gone from sceptic to passionate fan.

There is very little that cannot be done in XSLT. **I now rate it as my Number 1 tool for data manipulation.**"

Angus Scott-Knight
SAP-Primavera Integration Guru

As long as one does not fall into this marketing trap, exactly this long and deliberately complex sentence points at where the biggest fun with EPC comes in.

Extending EPC. Rid yourself of the notion that some ominous EPC template can be installed and function as a rugged, robust and sophisticated "interface" at the same time. Disregard any notion that the sheer ability to change a few mappings on the fly means flexibility and short implementation times.

Do that, but welcome the scalability of XSLT, the extendibility of the platform, of custom API calls, custom logic. Appreciate the ability to tailor a solution to exactly your process, using pre-packaged components and capabilities. Say yes to the open world of customized definition of workflows and logical steps and object-level mappings.

As long as you follow a mature methodology, implementations will be successful, and for the geeks in and of us, even fun! The above are the tools used, but the real reason for this fun is because they help putting smiles on the faces of customers. This is not meant to sound cheesy, although it probably does. It is my main indicator of success for implementations when an end-user touches a unit-tested system for the first time, or when I leave. (There could be lots of reasons for a smile, but hey - whatever it takes.)

An Emerging Ecosystem. It gets better, though. Not only does EPC offer the ability to tailor SAP-Primavera solutions to a client's specific process and functional and technical requirements. SAP has also triggered a process where the partner ecosystem steps in and addresses whatever above was mentioned as (to-be-expected) shortcomings.

Just look at the company I am working for, CEI. We offer pre-packaged components that can rapidly be deployed, that reduce risk, add commonly required features and functions.

My Conclusion. Go with SAP EPC. It's as simple as that.

Why not... Inspire?

A true story may help to understand my reasoning.

About a decade ago an Indian engineering and construction firm founded by engineers from Denmark built an in-house solution to link their SAP and Primavera applications. This was to resolve an internal pain point that many customers still feel today.

Realizing that this was a common challenge, they then attempted to commercialize it. Soon they were in bed with Primavera and shortly after the product was integrated into Primavera's product offering as "Inspire". Then Primavera wanted to expand on it and initiated a substantial re-engineering effort to make Inspire more scalable.

The product brought to light by then was based on SAP's XI (later called PI, now SI) enterprise application integration product, using SAP's WebDynpro user interface.

Oracle acquired Primavera, and now Oracle offers an SAP-Integration product that is almost solely based on SAP technology. In the meantime SAP acquired a much more streamlined product, integrated it into its technical landscape and greatly enhanced it.

The moral of the story? Oracle-Primavera tries to compete with SAP by using SAP technology and using a less capable and more complicated product as such.

The resulting product is at best en par, but mostly inferior in almost any aspect that counts for an industrial-strength solution. How could it compete with the dramatic flexibility and scalability of XSLT? With a process almost 100% of the time naturally beginning and ending in SAP ECC, why would one not want to use SAP authorization features, SAP logs, SAP transactions, or even SAP-based performance enhancement capabilities?

There are no advantages I can detect. Not even the vendor has a higher appeal, since Oracle and SAP arguably are similar in their often overbearing behavior as the major ERP application vendors of the planet.

Inspire does not eliminate the bottleneck of a relatively slow Primavera API. It does not make mappings easier, but more difficult to maintain. It does not eliminate infrastructure components and therefore the overall technical systems landscape. In the opposite, by using SAP's technology, and a platform that is considered inferior by SAP internally to address the task at hand, it confuses and complicates procurement, support, and technical considerations.

Integration into the Primavera API and Primavera database is not an argument for Inspire either. There is no special capability or performance advantage one would get with Inspire. Like the other few tools on the market it uses the Primavera API as the best-performing avenue of integration.

Functionality-wise, Primavera people are not usually SAP ERP experts. SAP ECC is a far more complex and complicated application than Primavera. It is a much bigger application also, and even in a Primavera-centric integration scenario it provides at a minimum half or more of the data required to deliver comprehensive project management capabilities, i.e. budgeted, planned, committed and actual costs; actual hours; resources; materials; procurement; or high-level project structures.

Primavera consultants are not natural integration consultants. Years after Primavera's acquisition by Oracle their ecosystem still seems full of professionals understanding Primavera's capabilities very well, but little about many aspects of backend-integrated organizational project management. EPC's ecosystem is comprised much more of people who know how to deal with complexities of the ERP world, who know how to maximize performance and streamline overall functionality instead of treating implementations primarily as a mapping exercise.

One could argue about success stories here or there. Yes, with enough time, cost and effort almost any mature EAI product can be used to build some interface that works reasonably well, including Inspire. That just proves overall competence, but does not make a case based on scope, cost, time, quality or risk of such an implementation.

I am also not saying that this is a bad product in and of itself, or that it cannot deliver. It just smells too much like a "me too" product for Oracle, kept on the product list due to it having come with the Primavera acquisition, and because it adds another revenue opportunity to Oracle for a relatively little continued investment, while keeping SAP on its toes.

My final argument is that on a more general level Oracle does probably not really care, as long as some integration product is being used. The implementation and use of any integration product will result in Primavera being made an integral part of an otherwise SAP-centric enterprise. This gives Oracle enough of a beachhead to push other product suites, particularly related ones like portfolio management solutions, or business analytics and intelligence products.

On the other hand, neither for SAP nor Primavera this is a big deal revenue-wise. Some organizations may initially be turned off when hearing about the price tag associated with SAP's EPC product. The fact is, though, that it is a relatively competitive price for an overall superior product.

My Conclusion. The Oracle Inspire product does not have any advantage over SAP's EPC product. Its use of SAP technology that SAP considers inferior to its own integration offering is a negative since it complicates its use on several levels. The higher flexibility of the XSLT-based middleware component of SAP EPC, and its better integration into the SAP back-end and technology landscape are overall advantages.

Therefore I see slight advantages in several areas for SAP EPC, and none for Inspire.

Why not... Pipeline?

This is a somewhat difficult one, but only due to personal reasons. The Pipeline integration product was acquired from one of my previous businesses, Intech Professionals. So naturally I have a great affinity for the product, which is in principle well-designed. Of course, since then it has greatly matured and been enhanced. Nowadays it is called Maxavera, for reasons that are explained below.

Pipeline's team is very capable. They know what they are doing and I respect the team around Charlie Sundling a lot. Cor Ruiten, Raju Patel, Jess Regal and the rest are great guys. The product is good. Purely functionality-wise and even considering SAP's whole ecosystem it would possibly still be competitive.

Maybe SAP should have acquired it instead of SOA Logix. Maybe not.

It all does not matter. The game is over and has been for a while.

For today's SAP-Primavera integration market, Pipeline's Maxavera is a niche product provided by a small company. Once the SAP EPC platform had matured and add-on capabilities and templates were enhancements and accelerators were available on the market, the competitive aspects mostly shift to areas where SAP has huge natural advantages.

The biggest questions now turn into support for multiple platforms, consistency of architecture, the scalability of the ecosystem, and the level of support one can get from the more complex solution. What SAP NetWeaver supports, EPC supports, and SAP has a very serious commitment to NetWeaver.

Pipeline may do lot of that also, or even be compatible with NetWeaver, but they require a separate interface, separate database tables, and their R&D and support efforts have to be spread to cover other interfaces also.

In one very specific circumstance Pipeline's has one advantage, though. The company does not define its product as a pure SAP-Primavera integration product (or SAP-MS Project integration product, which SAP-EPC also is). Its positioning is as an integration product for the asset management realm in general. The most extreme case would be integrating Primavera or MS Project into Maximo.

Could SAP EPC do that also? Of course it could. It is based on an EAI platform also.

But would it? Also of course this is unlikely, and if it were only due to Maximo and SAP PM being competitive products.

Therefore, the only substantial niche for Pipeline's integration product is with clients that use both SAP PM and Maximo, and design standard maintenance and outage management processes independent of both Maintenance Management Systems (MMS), with scheduling aspects in both cases centered on Primavera.

Even then, though, I would question some of the premises here. First, I see the integration of SAP PM and Maximo into the rest of the SAP ECC backend as much more critical than how dates will be calculated and progress will be reported when performing maintenance processes. EPC still can play a role here.

My Conclusion. In almost all circumstances this is a hands-down advantage for SAP. With the possible exception of customers pursuing a long-term strategy to support both SAP PM and Maximo as Maintenance Management Systems integrated with Primavera, Pipeline's integration product has no real place anymore when it comes to an enterprise selecting an integration product for the long-term. I would still put them at the number two spot. For that to be a serious consideration the number one has to seriously slip up, though, and I just don't see that happen right now.

Why not... Impress?

Every once in a while one encounters Impress Software when looking for integration solutions between SAP and Primavera. In most markets Impress is not seen as a competitive product anymore, although it still seems to have some foothold in some markets like the Middle East. The reason why I mention it here is primarily because of its history and because there are still a number of Impress solutions in service today.

So here comes another history lesson, with valuable learnings for anybody who tries to integrate enterprise business applications.

Impress was good enough while their run lasted, but that is mostly ancient history in the technology world. Their solution had a reputation for being a monster of an application with gigantic overhead, slow performance, difficult to maintain, and due to that very long implementation times and significant costs.

This reputation was factually correct, but some of the above criticism and reputation did them some injustice. Just after the turn of the century, when Impress developed the first widely sold Primavera integration product, they had correctly identified a big pain point in the market. Fueled by an aggressive marketing and sales effort, their product became synonymous with SAP-Primavera integration.

Then it fell apart. They simply had overextended themselves, were burdened with old technology.

A main underlying reason for success and failure seems to have been timing. At around 1999 and 2000 I attended a workshop of SAP in Toronto together with one of my key developers at Intech Professionals. There, the PS development team pushed for the development of a SAP-Primavera integration application. We showed a simple proof-of-concept that was mostly based on file uploads and downloads. But particularly Primavera was not ready yet, having not yet brought to market their Java API. So we decided to not (yet) pursue the building of a product.

At that time it had only been a couple of years that SAP had come out with a formal API, the Primavera client-server "enterprise" product was just about to seriously enter the market, and the Primavera Java API was not yet available. When Impress entered that market they had to compensate for many such deficiencies, and among others consider such big no-nos as directly accessing the Primavera database. Their overall solution was to use proprietary technology and a middleware database where the "truth" of all project structure data was kept. Data transfers were not real-time but respectively updated the middleware database.

This was not a sustainable solution. Projects went over budget, timelines were not met, performance was awful and the company went belly up and was eventually bought out by their founder. The word on the street is that the main motivation was to keep supporting their maintenance base. However, Impress's solutions have at least to some degree been rewritten and their integration products are still marketed.

They are not a dominant player in the overall SAP-Primavera market anymore, despite the fact that they occasionally they keep popping up. Mostly Impress' early customers are replacing the product, or at least exploring options to do so. I have been involved in a couple of these exercises.

My Conclusion. This is a "has-been" product offered by what nowadays is a niche player. Reputation of historic technical, implementation and corporate failures weigh heavily on the company. Having all of that said one should keep in mind that they have a lot of experience to deliver functioning integration in a mature market. I doubt that enough of the brain drain of senior personnel could be replaced to keep them as a viable option. When offerings like SAP EPC, Oracle Inspire, or Pipeline Maxavera are available, Impress cannot hold its own anymore.

Why not... SAP PI?

Most organization's IT departments wonder at least initially, "What about SAP PI? We have used it as an integration platform, it is an SAP product, we have expertise, and we don't want to add clutter in the form of just another integration platform like SAP EPC."

This is an interesting proposition. It definitely seems well-motivated and sounds logical on the surface. And certainly it should be possible to build a capable SAP-Primavera integration solution using any mature EAI product, including SAP PI. Considering how Primavera's Inspire had originally been marketed as an integration product built on PI, therefore even actively been pushed by SAP until Oracle acquired it, adds more spice to the story.

Then, however, think again.

Exactly that last point, of the Oracle Inspire product using SAP PI, hints at the great weakness of the above argument. If you really want to use PI, why not use Oracle's Inspire? You may say that I just above have made a fairly conclusive argument about Inspire not being able to match EPC's overall capabilities, and it falling short.

Surely using PI while working around Inspire's shortcomings would enable your business to end up with a mature product using a consistent EAI platform, specifically adapted to your specific needs. In theory, yes, but reality is more ugly. Just look at Inspire, as the product built with probably millions or dollars over the period of about a decade.

Granted, you don't want to build a marketable product. You just want to effectively address a pain point. However, it is difficult and costly to build a fully capable integration platform using PI. One has to add adapters for Primavera, add selection criteria, user-friendly logs and error handling, flexible mapping features, and all of that in a hopefully nimble enough manner to address a number of complex business requirements.

It is no surprise that SAP itself does not recommend using PI. Acknowledging the challenges with PI in this context is exactly the reason why they acquired SOA Logix and turned their product into EPC. Aspects like nimbleness, performance, usability are just too critical for the integrated schedule. EPC and its ever more established little ecosystem of enhancements and advanced features have so much knowledge and understanding of project management baked-in that it is unrealistic to expect one could reach comparable capabilities with a reasonable effort.

Keep also in mind that in the first step above I mentioned what should be the main driver for integrating SAP and Primavera: It is to offer a strategic enabler for enterprise projects to flexibly react to changing business situations, facilitating their effective execution of corporate strategy.

The deeper you dig, the more the logic toward PI falls apart.

Should my above points not be satisfactory enough, feel free trying to get to the ground of them. Maybe you discover something SAP or other companies have not seen. I doubt it.

My Conclusion. Building a solution using SAP PI may in theory be possibly, but in reality it is not a viable option. PI is lacking key solution components that would need to be developed from ground up, which EPC not only already has addressed. EPC's ecosystem has already developed enough add-on capabilities to render a re-inventing of the wheel approach using PI a non-starter.

Why not... other platforms?

Now that all major products have been analyzed and found wanting, confirming my choice of SAP EPC as the default product to pick, here comes the "PI question with a twist". If not SAP PI as an EAI platform, does this really mean no other EAI product should be considered to build a SAP-Primavera integration solution?

What about any other API product? For example TIBCO? Doesn't Gartner say that it is the market leader in "On-Premise Application Integration" and a leader as a "Business Intelligence and Analytics Platform"? Shouldn't that mean that an integration solution built using this platform would be industry-leading while also providing instantaneous reporting and analytical capabilities?

Theoretically, maybe. In reality the answer is in almost all respects similar to my above analysis of SAP PI as a potential integration platform. Who has done it before? And why is it not being pursued?

The main argument against this thinking is that the whole premise is upside down. Integrating SAP and Primavera is not primarily a technical challenge. Yes, we all know that it comes down to code. Good developers and good money and the right team and enough time can achieve wonderful things.

However, knowledge about SAP-Primavera integration is not a commodity. Only few people have dug down deeply and figured it out and done it. This required a senior-level and experienced and skillful team and vision.

Replicating this is not easy and can be very risky.

The question should therefore not be whether it can be done. Sure it can. It should be why one would risk time, money and success to Build vs. Buy. Above in my description of the tactical parameters for implementing a solution I have strongly argued for buying a platform, buying advanced solution components, and buying expertise, as opposed to building all of that from scratch. I am sticking to that.

One should ask oneself whether there really are good arguments not going with a packaged and proven product. If you figure them out, please let me know.

I simply cannot come up with any.

My Conclusion. Don't try to build and re-invent something that already exists in a mature and proven state, particularly when there are no obvious cost benefits but substantial risks.

(3) Consider Additional Tool Requirements

Build vs. Buy - Again

So far I talked about the integration platform to be used, and it pretty much came down to SAP EPC. The selection of tools does not stop there, though. Instead of building solutions from scratch, you can leverage existing capabilities available in the EPC ecosystem. This reduces risk, shortens delivery times, reduces overall costs, provides for better supportability, and leverages mature developments that in almost all cases will handily beat any ad-hoc development effort you could engage in.

This is the world of accelerators, add-ons, features, functions, and enhancements. This is like with your smart phone, which is a great platform and even comes with a few apps. The real value comes with the apps, and when leveraging what is becoming an ever more capable ecosystem.

Now, EPC surely is no iPhone or Galaxy. It is an SAP product, but I hope you still get my drift.

In the following, let me point out a few examples for additional tools that enhance the EPC platform. These have all been developed as internal R&D efforts using the systems environment and professional capabilities of CEI, short for Competitive Edge International, Inc. (www.cei-corp.com). They are based on common requirements that were identified during a large number of implementations throughout the past 15 years.

CEI offers these enhancements and add-ons as "accelerators" that are seamlessly integrated into the core EPC platform. This means there is a one-time charge associated with them, but no maintenance. During an implementation, these tools become an integral part of the overall solution.

Of course you could also completely discard the thought of reusing proven concepts and solutions. But then we would be back to the pros and cons of re-inventing the wheel, or the concept of writing...

API Enhancements

The Challenge. What do you do if you need to interact with fields that are not part of standards BAPIs? What do you do if you need to create objects from Primavera in SAP that are not inherently supported by the standard SAP API? How do you more efficiently interact with ranges of objects in SAP? How do you show the SAP descriptions for IDs that are not intuitive to Primavera users? How do you combine API calls from and into different modules of SAP?

The Answer. Advanced BAPIs cover the basic functionality of standard BAPIs, combine them, enhance them, and add the ability to interact with a large number of additional data elements. They support, among others:

- Custom fields,
- The creation of WBS elements from Primavera,
- The creation of Activities from Primavera,
- The pulling of HR master records from SAP,

- The pulling of Statistical Key Figures from SAP,
- The pulling of vendor-related data from SAP,
- The pulling of sales-related data from SAP,
- The creation of budget numbers in SAP, or
- Changes of user and system statuses in SAP.

Beyond the above, CEI's advanced APIs also contain lookup function that render names to IDs like cost centers, profit centers, of functional locations. This addresses limitations of standard SAP BAPIs. Enhanced BAPIs are more performance optimized that standard ones by limiting the number of calls to the SAP backend. They also return additional performance metrics.

These BAPIs support the interaction with PS and PM, although they also incorporate capabilities from other modules of SAP, like HR, MM or SD. They go in concert with related XSLT code components that are built to interact with these BAPIs.

Conditional Updates Engine

The Challenge. How can I prevent data from being overwritten every single time? How can I introduce advanced logical conditions that are based on the state of fields in one or the other of the applications? How can I introduce such logical conditions for a group of mappings?

The Answer. CEI's Conditional Updates Engine contains the ability to real-time compare data from SAP and Primavera and add logic based on the results of this comparison. Its practical use has few limits, and it is a key tool to achieve many of the typically required logical conditions during an implementation.

On the lowest level it allows to include logical conditions like create-only or update-only rules, by field.

More intricate are conditions like "if this Primavera UDF says 'Green', change the status in SAP to Release, if it is 'Red' change the status in SAP to Technically Complete".

Among the more complex capabilities are the introduction of parameters in Primavera that introduce controls over mappings. An example would be an indicator like "transfer relationships only if this indicator is set to 'Yes'".

I have not seen a solution that I would consider robust, industrial-strength and genuinely enterprise-ready, except when conditional updates were used.

Transfer Management

The Challenge. How can I stop and start transfers that potentially slow down the system or even lead to data integrity issues? In complex scenarios how can I prevent having to rerun full transfers to address a small number of errors? How do I best determine how to optimize batch sizes and use multi-threading?

The Answer. As the name says, Transfer Management introduces a number of capabilities for the more granular management of transfers. This includes the ability to:

- Stop transfers anytime
- Start transfers anytime
- See transfer progress and numbers of errors
- Re-process errors only
- Interactively view detailed performance metrics split

It also introduces additional capabilities to optimize performance of transfers, by adding the ability to:

- Create custom logs to better interpret processing issues
- Dynamically change batch sizes
- Dynamically change numbers of threads

The above gives users full control and visibility of transfers as required in real-life. This solution component often works hand-in-hand the with more advanced transfer simulation, error handling and transfer reports capabilities of CEI's Synchronization Manager.

Performance Optimizer

The Challenge. How can one noticeably or even dramatically limit the number of API calls that EPC has to make? How can one achieve an improvement in performance by up to a factor of ten times or more as compared to "regular" transfers?

The Answer. The Performance Optimizer is an ABAP add-on that helps limit the number of objects selected in SAP to those that have been changed since the last update. Through this the performance of transfers can be optimized by a huge factor.

Through the ability to dramatically improve the selection of data, combined with optimized API calls, optimized transfer batching and threading, and the use of the conditional updates engine and smart logic, EPC is able to synchronize tens of thousands of activities within an hour.

One recent client set performance goals of "15,000 activities in 10 minutes". We did it.

Transfer Simulation

The Challenge. Is it possible to see in advance what the result of transfers would be, including errors or logical issues? How can I figure out whether my manual data conversion activity has been successful or not, without having to run a potentially error-laden transfer?

The Answer. The Transfer Simulation covered by the CEI Synchronization Manager provides the ability to get a picture of the results of transfers without having to run them. Detailed logs point out data inconsistencies, or errors, or changes to data.

Users can run these simulations in advance and correct issues even before they reach the target system.

One of the most significant uses of this tool is when data has to be manually manipulated, e.g. as part of a data conversion effort.

Custom Error Handling

The Challenge. How can a end-user or support person find out the exact reason for an error or warning triggered by a transfer? How can error codes or logical conditions be explained in commonly understandable English sentences so that one does not need to sift through lengthy and cryptic error logs?

The Answer. As part of CEI's Synchronization Manager tool, error messages can be captured and displayed with more meaningful sentences in plain English. Without the need to resort to lengthy technical error logs, the user, or a functional support person can interpret the issues and initiate steps to correct them.

This capability is critical for custom implementations, particularly when you apply complex logic conditions and rules during transfers.

Resource Transfers

The Challenge. How can I enable Primavera to assign resources, particularly such that may not yet have been associated with previous project activities? How can I reflect changes in the resource hierarchy? How can I consider status changes of SAP resources? How can I transfer a complete SAP resource hierarchy into Primavera, and keep it synchronized? How can I get individual HR master records into Primavera?

The Answer. Independent of project resources (project work centers or project HR resources), a generic resources transfer brings across all resources in a certain selection. It pulls the work center resources hierarchy, and rebuilds it in case of subsequent changes. SAP Work Centers are brought over as labor resources or roles. Individuals are pulled from SAP HR Master Records based on their assignment to SAP Work Centers.

Locked or inactive resources can be excluded from transfers, or set as inactive in Primavera also.

This tool is indispensable if you desire to give Primavera control over resource assignments to activities.

Custom Transactions

The Challenges. How do I prevent orphaned orders due to inconsistent selections (e.g. order ranges selecting orders that are not in scope of a revision)? How to I keep users focused on relevant selections of work only? How do I introduce specific project-level mappings?

The Answer. You need to use a custom transaction that addresses the above challenges. Custom transactions introduce project-level mappings like:

- SAP Revision = P6 Project
- SAP Project = P6 Project
- SAP WBS = P6 Project
- SAP Functional Location = P6 Project

These contain pre-defined selections and "missing order" catching logic. Such logic informs schedulers when data inconsistencies have been discovered in the course of transfers.

Solution Templates

Based on a large number of outage and turnaround management processes, CEI has put together several templates for the management of typically integrated business processes. One of these is the OMS, or Outage Management Solution, combining a representative process flow and related required advanced features and functions.

This solution template incorporates many of the proven functions and features, as well as typical mappings and logic capabilities, performance enhanced, using the conditional updates engine, interacting with the enhanced API, and triggered through a user friendly custom transaction with simulation and custom error handling features.

The solution is in the default based on revisions as the key selection and project-level mapping criterion.

The Outage Management Solution template is best used:

A. For demonstrations of EPC capabilities and contributions to manage turnarounds and outages;
B. As a close-to-life reference during scoping and detailed design efforts; and
C. As a template to start out the rapid deployment and refinement of a prototype or solution.

The Outage Management Solution comes with pre-specified process assumptions, pre-defined business scenarios, and with a specific set of Primavera layouts and reports.

4.

WHO? PICK THE RIGHT TEAM

Not a Commodity

Whatever you get out of the following, above all keep in mind that skill and knowledge of SAP-Primavera integration is not a commodity. Experience is key. Very few people or even organizations, though, have knowledge, skill, an experience.

Not to despair, though, your solution is simple.

We are at Step 4 towards the Integrated Schedule. You have clarified your strategic goals, have set realistic strategic parameters and picked the right tools. Now it is time to pick the right team. Selecting the right people is key as with any other business activity. The team needs to be skillful, experienced, balanced, well led, focused, professional and jive well with each other. When working with the team members you also need to consider know-how transfer, support, and rollout.

Frequently I see a knee-jerk reaction to go out on the market looking for an "EPC Consultant". (See Myth 5, below) Then LinkedIn is lighting up, and recruiters start calling. Then frustration sets in, and eventually one compromises, picks just about anybody who has been around one of such projects before, asks SAP Labs for installation help and guidance, and embarks on a sometimes quite long and painful journey.

The need of an "EPC Consultant" is one of the most misleading concepts and can set one up for failure, or at least set the stage for a compromised and dissatisfying sub-par solution.

On the other hand it can be so "easy". If you have followed step one above and have secured a realistic budget based on a solid business case, then go ahead focusing on the job and not on developing in-house know-how and experience first. Buy the services of the right team of outside experts at a fixed price, complement it with internal skilled personnel, perform the implementation together, and through that process gain the in-house expertise to continue supporting the solution and embark on realistic next phases, should that be required.

"EPC Consulting" is not a commodity. Neither is SAP-Primavera integration consulting. There are no large numbers of experts around. Even more, there are hardly any people on the market that would be able to cover most of the knowledge, know-how and experience. The various skills required are too different and the overall number of global implementations is too small for that.

Besides the relatively small number of SAP-Primavera integration projects using EPC, there are much easier ways of earning a living for a professional. You could be a project management expert, solution architect, a PS or ENC or Capital Projects or PPM consultant, a PM or EAM consultant, an ABAP developer, an XSLT developer, a Primavera scheduler or Primavera consultant, or SAP Basis consultant. Why bother with the complicated stuff? For the average professional, such a project may be an exciting change, but chances are that it will be years before one encounters another one.

The typical IT and business application consultant is skilled, but narrowly so. Dealing with cross-application functionality, processes and technologies is a different ballgame. Even terminology may be an issue. What is the role of a WBS in Primavera vs. SAP? What is a budget? What are non-labor resources? Or Calendars? How do scheduling parameters here affect those in the other application? What is "status" again, and who is being an "EPS"?

On top of this, another aspect is learning the logic of how an integrated process flow needs to work, and related pros and cons. In that context, functionality is only one challenge, even though it means that even simple test scenarios require working in both applications hand in hand. Understanding and logically approaching a complete project life-cycle goes far beyond understanding technical functionality or how to install, configure or set up SAP PS, PM or Primavera.

Translating all of the above into a supportable solution, that is the key challenge.

With all respect to superbly skilled people, integration is a totally different animal. There are not many knowledgeable consultants around, and even far less that have been exposed to it more than one or two times in their professional careers. That is why the right outside expert team is critical to one's ability to not just implement "something", but to implement a scalable and internally supportable solution.

So it comes down again to picking the right people.

On the next pages I will explain how to do exactly that.

The Value of Outside Experts

During a 100 m run, my son can reach 80% of the speed of Usain Bolt. That does not quite make him win races yet...

It is similar when it comes to integrating schedules across applications.

Skill. Experience. Know-how.

That about sums it about. But just in case there are any questions, let me say it in a few hundred words more.

Don't fall for the big company that says they are experts in everything. Smart people alone do not ensure good software or good projects. Nobody can be good at everything.

On the other extreme, don't fall for the individual who has been part of a team before, just because it sounds like they did something similar. Chances are that "similar" thing was in reality "unique" in some way. How could it be otherwise, with every ERP environment set up so differently? Businesses work differently, and the devil is in the detail.

Also, don't let self-proclaimed "experts" tell you they have the skills and know it all. Let them prove it to you. Ask the below questions, let them show you, and then select based on what you see.

There is a huge difference between knowledge and experience, and even between knowhow and experience. That is not to say that skills, knowledge and knowhow are not necessary and critical ingredients of a good team. It just says that these are not sufficient. For example, I know Primavera pretty well, but am I the expert I would trust key solution design decision with, in a complex business environment? Hardly.

There is no definite "best practice" when it comes to complete solutions, only "proven practices". Each business is unique in its own way, although most project management processes have of course lots of similarities also.

Here is how to evaluate an implementation team:

- Have they done it before? How many times? Working with each other?
- Can they demonstrate solutions? Live? Complex ones? Enhanced ones? Variations and beyond "out-of-the-box" samples?
- Do they have accelerators and tools?
- How vested are they in SAP-Primavera integration? Is it a focus of their business? Do they engage in R&D related to that subject, develop enhancements, packaged solutions, add-ons?
- Do they have their own environments? SAP ECC, Primavera P6, SAP EPC, potentially multiple servers?

- Have they delivered solutions for the processes you address (Outages, Capital, Make-to-Order)?
- Do they have the full range of skills required?
- Do they have references and success stories?
- Can they tell you what worked and what didn't?
- What were their biggest challenges?
- Are they willing to put their money where their mouth is?
- Do they know what they don't know, and are they willing to admit it?

When you have the answers to the above you will know whether the team is right. Check your cost-benefit analysis, ensure you have the budget, hire them and get going. Don't waste time and money. Don't agonize about such a decision. Engage real experts when you encounter them.

6 Key Recommendations

My assumption in the following is that the EPC product has been picked as the integration platform. The core of the below input would also apply to alternative platforms, but some of the specifics I mention relate to EPC only.

1. Cover All Core Skills and Roles

My first recommendation is to ensure all skills are represented and involved in a project. Such a skill is not just to be the narrow technical or functional "know-how". When delivering a SAP-Primavera Integration Solution, every area of expertise needs to be represented by a person who has a very good understanding of the overall process and of all tactical parameters outlined above. It cannot be a silo. During an implementation you need sometimes unexpectedly complex solutions, questions raised, assumptions challenged, specifications interpreted, unit tests performed, and individual tasks put in the overall context.

Following is a breakdown of the skills required and the expectations for the people delivering them. Sometimes the same person can play two or three roles, but in general it helps looking at them as separate roles that need to be individually sourced.

The Business. Here I am not talking about a functional expert or a scheduler. I mean the manager or owner of a business process who understands what happens throughout a project, from start to finish, and what standardized processes are in place or are about to be implemented. This person is also responsible for ensuring sufficient input from other business units if applicable, and for potential change management and training efforts. This is the person who should drive the overall solution design, and who will make functional design decisions. He or she is the equivalent or representative of the main customer of the integration solution.

The PMO. This may be the same person as "the business", particularly since sometimes project management is a generic and standardized skill across the organization. As the "project management organization", the PMO contributes knowledge and ownership of corporate standardized project management practices and tools. In that context, a PMO can be even more critical than the business - if it has the proven ability to transfer the theoretical and formal ownership of standard processes and tools into the real-life of various business units.

Functional: Overall Solution Design. Somebody needs to be able to pull the entire functional design requirements together, while considering the technical, process and organizational context, and translate the business requirements into a consistent and practical functional design. This role contributes by defining pros and cons, or pointing out options and forcing decisions. It is a key liaison between the business and the technical team members.

Technical: Installation. Although this is very specialized, it is not the simplest one even for an experienced person. EPC installation can be extremely straightforward, or extremely complex, and anything in-between. Beyond specifics of EPC, in principle this person should understand aspects of server administration, security, authentication and authorization (e.g. LDAP), and the installation and management of databases,

NetWeaver, the Primavera API, and the Primavera Database. It may also require an appreciation of complexities relating to remote access, VPN or hosted environments. And yes, to be able to validate an installation's success, a good basic understanding of functionality helps also.

Programming: ABAP. This is for the extension of the SAP API, for performance optimization. Don't misinterpret its contribution as a pure adding of a field here or there. And don't underestimate the value of experience here also. Not just any ABAP developer can add sufficient value. The specific ABAP expert needs to understand the impact on mappings, performance, error handling, supportability of the overall solution, for example.

Programming: XSLT. In EPC this is where the solution is tailored to reflect functional requirements. This person does not just need to understand how to code XSLT, but how to do it in the context of EPC, how the Primavera API and the SAP BAPI layer work, how performance may be impacted, how advanced capabilities like conditional updates are best reflected. And again, experience matters big time, as solution recommendations need to be seen in the big context and should be put in perspective of past engagements of a similar kind.

Functional: Primavera. Almost in all integration projects I have been involved in Primavera users, i.e. schedulers and planners, were the most directly impacted by the solution, maybe apart from people analyzing progress, earned value and costs.

A Primavera functional expert will design reports and layouts, set up codes and user-defined fields, contribute to decisions about the setting up of resource hierarchies, provide input on functional implications of data flows, guide through status management and scheduling processes. A functional Primavera integration expert will be instrumental during the definition of unit test and integration test scenarios, assist during the analysis and definition of logical conditions to be reflected in mappings, and provide input to performance optimization tasks.

At times integration projects are triggers to implement Primavera, or to upgrade it, or to consolidate multiple environments into one. This may then require solution design and functional and administrative tasks, data cleansing, documentation, or training.

Functional: SAP PS and/or PM. During the cause of the implementation a number of questions about specific processes are likely to pop up, to be answered by functional experts. They do not just have to understand the generic capabilities of these modules, but also how they specifically are reflected in the wider business context. At times they may also required to perform configuration changes, e.g. by adding new user-defined fields or control keys, or the like.

Some of the job of a functional SAP expert is also to be able to set up representative test data, or even replicate configuration and representative data in the service provider's environment.

Project Management. This role is so critical that I reserved a full set of recommendations for it. See below, recommendation number 6.

2. Ensure Supporting Roles are Covered

While the above are absolutely critical to be able to deliver the solution's capabilities and requirements, there are a number of functions that need to be included and considered. One big difference is that they do not necessarily need to have a detailed upfront understanding of the integration functionality or scope, and don't need integration-specific experience.

"Supporting" roles mostly means "less frequently important" roles. I have specific experiences for how each one of the below has at times been on the critical path of a project, and how delays in support have led to delays in the delivery of core project tasks.

Technical: Network. This includes supporting that the system landscape is connected properly and data can flow. It also may involve the monitoring of network performance. Another contribution is to provide network access to external personnel, potentially involving fob keys and remote access.

Technical: Basis System. A typical SAP-Primavera integration project will require Basis system support on several levels. Apart from authorizations (addressed in the next bullet), this refers to the installation of SAP NetWeaver, the installation of the ABAP component of EPC code, the installation of enhanced or changed RFCs, and of add-on components. Some of these tasks will need to be repeated in development, test, pre-production and production environments. Others may require the frequent and rapid initiation of transports to support test and fix cycles. At times a Basis System expert may also be called on to analyze performance issues, or to address database or other system settings in SAP ECC.

Technical: SAP Authorization. SAP EPC and the various team members need to have proper authorizations to connect the EPC application, while the project team needs to be able to perform unit and integration tests. Both require authorizations. During development this may be admin-level privileges. Having those can be particularly important at the beginning of a project. Later, introducing more narrow SAP authorizations is likely a necessary condition for going live.

Technical: Hardware. This role addresses the procurement and setup of hardware and related operating systems. This can be on the critical path and should be addressed before the actual project start. During the project, and particularly while optimizing performance, hardware availability and optimization may play a role again, and support and active participation in the project may be required.

Technical: Primavera Installation. This function may get involved only during the initial setup of environments (development, test, pre-production, production), or also potentially during performance optimization efforts, or to tune the database or address technical issues relating to the Primavera Database or Primavera API.

Functional: Other SAP Modules. Here I need to stay general because it depends on the specific context and the specific functional specifications of the solution. A Primavera-SAP integration solution may involve the interaction with human resources (HR) or human capital management (HCM), sales (SD), procurement (MM), or even production planning (PP), investment management (IM) or portfolio management (PPM). Typically such contributions are on an ad-hoc basis.

3. Mix Experience with Skills

Individual skills are not everything one should ask from a team. Rather, also ensure that you put together an experienced expert implementation team that combines all core capabilities. Three words should stick out: "experienced", "expert", and "all". It is not good enough to just get general exposure or skills in some of the areas described below.

The balance can make or break it. Without skills or without experience, one will fall short. However, one does not need to double up with experienced internal and external resources. A proven practice is to pair the experience of outside experts with internal skilled team members, ensuring the job can get done properly and know-how is transferred while minimizing falling into common traps.

Actually having done it makes a huge difference. Specifically having done it, multiple times, even more often. This is what I call "experience". For example, if you ask me whether an EPC installation expert and integration consultant like our own Gregory Richardson can install the Primavera database, or the Primavera API, or SAP NetWeaver, my answer is of course yes. If you ask me whether he is able to configure a Primavera application in a generic form, the answer also is yes.

However, if you are asking me whether he is an experienced expert in all of that, in specific areas my confidence level may be somewhat lower. I would then, and he would too, point at the extra value one can get from an expert having set up and implemented Primavera many times over. Somebody who has formal training, hands-on experience - plus actual experience with analyzing scheduling processes and detailed Primavera setup requirements, evaluating pros and cons of certain approaches, and recommending specific courses of action to achieve ones goals.

Expert skills are a requisite. They are not enough on such a level, though. Specific experience of skilled personnel matters.

The same applies to any of the core competencies required. A deficiency in just one of these aspects could impact the overall quality of the solution delivered. If a system is down for a few days or weeks, then everybody may be affected. So installation experience of a professional with expert skills - that is what helps.

At one client, at the beginning of an engagement I once was told in December that "EPC is installed and basically working". More than four months later, it really was installed and basically working. The difference were the word "almost", and many details.

The point here is not that it takes four months to install the EPC platform (it doesn't, can in good circumstances be done in a matter of a couple of days). Rather it is that often there are complexities and dependencies and decisions to be taken that one cannot see and anticipate and appreciate without experience, and that cannot be resolved easily without expert guidance.

4. Combine Internal Resources with Outside Experts

My fourth recommendation is to find a good balance between internal resources and outside experts. The goal here is to ensure a maximum level of know-how transfer without sacrificing the speed and quality of the deployment process, particularly in early stages of the project.

The below applies almost solely to the core skills and roles. Rarely will supporting roles need to be provided purely because an SAP-Primavera integration project is going on. However, if you know that there is a shortage of resources and a corresponding slow reaction time, address it early on.

A good mix between internal and external team members is important because outside experts usually bring experience, tools, and a very good appreciation of how the various skills, functional aspects and technical components are related and connected. This injection of experience and of a big picture perspective generally reduces risks and improves the quality of the solution.

The most important areas of outside expertise are installation, XSLT and ABAP, and functional Primavera knowledge. Here is where the external team usually drives the solution.

External expertise is necessary and sufficient to deliver technical and functional solution aspects. However, it cannot replace the know-how of internal experts that understand the specific setup, configuration, and standards of an organization's SAP or Primavera applications. They also cannot know specifics about data structures, data volumes, business requirements, or organizational idiosyncrasies.

What they can do is put this know-how in perspective and ensure that it is properly digested and reflected in a working solution. By pairing external with internal specialists, you can transfer know-how and move ever more expertise into the support organization.

For example, while external functional and process expertise can be particularly critical early in the implementation, it will eventually play a smaller role the closer one comes to testing in a production-like environment. Then representative test data needs to be set up, and test scenarios executed, for specifications that have been clearly described upfront. It is the point where internal functional and business specialists take over, and the contribution of external specialists will become much more sporadic.

The main takeaway from this section is that you should not try to trade internal skills with external ones. It is unrealistic, and often outright wrong, to assume that "we have ABAP developers", "we know Primavera functionality", "we have Primavera installed", "we have EPC installed", and "we have SAP functional expertise in-house". Such statements miss the point. There is a big-picture aspect, an efficiency, risk, and quality perspective, an experience gap, and a need to work at times with and in outside systems. It is not an "either - or", but both are required, although at different times with different degree of involvement.

Otherwise it becomes the precursor of the "all I need is an EPC consultant" statement (Myth 5), and the project blows up or becomes severely limited or delayed, wasting money and negating key benefits.

My experience with a number of implementations is that in all cases there was a mix of outside resources that showed up as a team, not as a group of individuals. The moment you try to pick and chose individuals to put your own core team together, the efficiency and effectiveness of the team goes down significantly. The balance between experience and skills does not work anymore, big picture aspects are missing, risks go up, quality goes down, and tensions rise. Often it may take until the testing phase before the majority of the issues become obvious to everybody.

And then - forget about seeing your end users and business owners smile...

What for, I may ask? Hopefully not to save a bit of money, because you will throw that one out the back door multiple times over when everybody needs to get up the learning curve the long and hard way.

5. Balance Technical, Functional, SAP and Primavera Skills

When LinkedIn requests start pouring in about the need for an "EPC Consultant', the implied requirement usually is "somebody who can show us how to make a few changes to the out-of-the-box EPC template". As if the "template" were more than a sample, and as if implementing EPC were a technical task.

It is not. Technical and functional skills need to be balanced. Implementations of SAP-Primavera integration solutions are not mapping exercises. Their goal is to link two powerful business applications. Therefore they also cannot rely solely on SAP or Primavera experts either, they need both.

Yes, I am repeating myself: It's the balance that makes it happen. The best and most effective professional teams in the world are small, no larger than a handful. Each team member is a specialist but each team member also understands enough about the other team's roles to contribute.

That's how it is done.

Ask yourself a few questions to process this properly:

- How many SAP Basis people know how to install NetWeaver and how to set up the Primavera API?
- How many ABAP developers do you know who also are experts in XSLT?
- How many ABAP or XSLT developers are also SAP or Primavera consultants?
- How many SAP consultants are also Primavera consultants?
- How many of any of those have real-life experience of full complex SAP-Primavera integrations?

The skills and experience needed are an understanding of project management principles and processes, integrated into an ERP back-end, and linked to a scheduling solution. A complete project life cycle is to be analyzed, and then it needs to be translated into technical requirements, implemented in code (ABAP and XSLT), tested and delivered.

Each requirement is to be defined, questioned, and refined. Implications of decisions are to be scrutinized, data is to be mocked up and processes and solutions are to be simulated. Then developers turn a proof of concept into a prototype, and eventually into the full solution. They then optimize performance and consider the end user in mind.

All these steps are not strictly sequential. They happen on every level in the project.

It's a well-balanced team.

Putting together the right team is what ensures project success. A failure to do so means having to compromise on quality and functionality, fall back on support from SAP, still fall short in many tasks, fail, delay, re-invent, muddle through, have communication failure, re-develop, more mud, something works, let's declare victory and move on.

No, let's do it right, have the users declare victory, and then move on.

6. Pick the Right Project Manager

Everybody is likely to agree that project management is a key ingredient of the SAP-Primavera integration project's success. I am adding this recommendation about the right project manager, and right project management approach, because I have seen projects stand and fall with it. Be too strict or too relaxed, and things are likely to get ugly. Come in too late, and things are likely to start ugly.

Let me point out some of the reason for ugliness.

(A) Too relaxed. In one of my first implementation projects there was hardly any tough project management. There was no drop-dead timeline, no high urgency to deliver the solution at any specific point in time. The implementation team worked off its own schedule, and things seemed to go well.

Deliverables were met, right until several times delays in critical path supporting functions (hardware, network access, etc.) led to multi-months interruptions of the project. To stop that, suddenly a solid timeline was established, the business expressed a newly-found urgency, and the pressure was on.

As the final sign-off came closer, the business discovered design shortcomings, consequently reflected in insufficient functionality. Retroactively specifications were adjusted, sign-off on deliverables revoked, double-work was pushed at the supplier and tensions rose.

Welcome ugliness (not).

My main learning is that project management must not be too relaxed. To deliver a workable solution, follow a proven methodology and enforce everybody's deadlines, involve the business early on and make them accountable. This makes deliverables and their sign off much more meaningful. Pressure should never get too high. It should be spread throughout the project, not pushed to the end.

Don't be too relaxed about project management.

(B) Too strict. The situation was quite the opposite in another implementation where I subcontracted with my team. SAP-Primavera integration being an unknown quantity, the main

team seemed pre-occupied with their standard implementation work. We were pulled in late, but developed a plan to catch up to the rest of the team.

Suddenly the overall project timeline was accelerated. There was silence for a few days, then all hell broke lose. We were asked to cut our core delivery time to one third (!), change our methodology, make additional resources available on a short notice, and work in a dysfunctional technical environment.

The project management style encountered here was uncompromising and deadlines were communicated top-down. Objections and suggestions for alternative ways of resolving the challenge were not considered, and "debunked" as self-serving, even though we had given a fixed price guarantee. It was project management by fiat.

Another kind of ugliness.

My main learning is that project managers in a project with such high complexity as ours should be facilitators above all. The main management challenge of such an integration project is the high number of moving parts (here is one of my favorite terms again). Those need to be aligned and kept moving. Strict or even aggressive top-down project management counters the whole premise of how to manage complex projects in a networked world.

Above all, though, be the enabling project manager, not the tense and aggressive one implying distrust about his team.

(C) Too late. Several times now I have fallen in the following trap, and I vow not to do it again: Starting to perform significant project work at risk. A challenge that we frequently encounter is that a business focuses on scope and evaluation of tools, takes a lot of time to deliberate, finally makes a decision, and everybody wants to continue the momentum and get going right away to reach an aggressive, and often artificial, timeline.

It's what I call the "hurry up and wait - are you done yet" mentality.

The big problem with that is that it cuts short the project preparation phase and puts individuals under pressure due to external factors. Primarily the availability of systems, dependencies on other vendors, and contractual relationships including specific payment terms and a completely mutually agreed statement of work are not considered yet.

This leads to big distractions on all team members. Some of the project work commences while another stalls, people don't get paid but work on a word, third parties supplying support services smell blood in the water and find justifications for a whole bunch of related and unrelated activities, actions, or lack thereof.

An ugliness of the third kind...

My main learning out of that is that the project manager should get involved immediately after the project decision has been made, if not even before that. He or she should make it the number one purpose to move the logistical issues out of the way, before formally involving any outside expert and kicking off core project activities.

Of course not all projects are created equally. Sometimes there is little time pressure and plenty of expertise around. I have seen this typically at implementations where SAP-Primavera integration is part of an initial SAP implementation lasting a year. In such circumstances it has proven to be best if the outside experts are authorized and sponsored to be supported wherever necessary, but otherwise by-and-large left alone. As long as they work in a disciplined manner, they get good support from the rest of the team, and can deliver. Let's admit it, a typical long-term SAP project has an abundance of resources and expertise available, which not always have the highest time pressure.

So, that can work well.

A Guideline. Here are some helpful rules about effective project manager's behavior in SAP-Primavera integration projects.

The below list is not supposed to replace the chapter about project management (Step 6). It is meant as a guideline for the professional behavior and actions of a project manager. A lot of it is based on two experiences with complex implementation projects I was involved in, at one of the world's major engineering companies and an African utility. Thanks Adrian Mendez! Thanks Dean Van Der Merwe!

- Facilitate communication wherever you can, but primarily between supporting staff and key team members.
- Ensure everybody has all means to work, including access to networks and systems.
- Take care of all logistics for workshops.
- Have weekly status meetings or calls.
- Distribute prompt and detailed results and action oriented meeting minutes.
- Keep a high-level project plan with all deliverables, but keep the lowest level tasks in a list of to do items so that the plan does not get overburdened with dependencies and the need for constant changes when updated.
- Trust your team and your team's judgment (questioning allowed!), or have them fired.
- Don't ever let questions remain unanswered or issues un-addressed.
- Keep a comprehensive issue list.
- Keep everybody accountable to his or her deliverables.
- Take on the responsibility to move through stage gates.
- Let the teamwork independently and don't micromanage.
- Ensure that all team members can cut through the thicket of technical, commercial and business formalities.
- Drive commercials and make sure they don't add pressure to any project team members.
- Ensure prompt sign off of project deliverables and milestones, pushing for immediate payments according to agreed-on conditions.
- Communicate. Up and down (and left and right, and forwards and backwards).
- Pay attention to details.

Related Challenges

The Systems Integrator (SI)

A fact of life and service delivery in large organizations is that this often involves "systems integrators" (SIs) as part of the larger team. Their role varies. I have mainly seen three kinds, listed here in sequence of "usually most contentious" to "usually least contentious":

(A) SIs being responsible for the overall execution of nothing but the SAP-Integration project itself. The argument behind this setup is that somebody needs to coordinate the supporting functions, and that SIs are predestined for such a job particularly if they can contribute a technical or functional resource or two also. Here the big question is the value-add of the SI's wider role. Are they effectively set up to perform a role to manage other vendors? Or are they mainly performing a project management role that quickly can be interpreted as sheer overhead?

(B) SIs being responsible for implementing business process standards and the related change management. This often involves their performing of business process analysis, process design, functional consulting including configuration of the SAP environment, documentation, and training. Examples for such processes relevant to SAP-Primavera integration may be the implementation of a portfolio management solution (PPM), or of an advanced enterprise asset management (EAM) solution, of a new module of SAP, or of Primavera.

In most of those examples there is little value added to have the SAP-Primavera project being run as a subset of the overall project. However, there can be value by having the process owner closely coordinating (or "project managing") that part of a related overall solution also.

(C) SIs performing the implementation of SAP. This results in the SAP-Primavera integration project being treated as a pure line item. Since such integration is usually done much faster than full-scale EPR implementations, these are in principle

low-risk projects. They can be straightforward wins for all sides. The client, and therefore also the SI as the one responsible for delivery, gets a potential headache taken care of. A special challenge may be the volatility of such projects, and that decision-makers from the business or SI side rarely have all the answers required for a final design.

Be aware that there are likely to be differences in the motivations of an SI and of the outside expert team. Those are usually rooted in a different engagement model (time and expense based vs. fixed price) that may impact the sense of urgency or the reaction to additional work requests.

It can be much cleaner to provide a clear division of the project management role and assigning it to competent individuals without further responsibilities. That is my default recommendation.

The Single "Expert"

Every so often I see at an SAP-Primavera integration project an internal or external "expert" involved who guides the organization through the process of defining the solution and steering through the implementation. Often this is a senior level business consultant, likely with some strong background in one of the technical or functional areas involved. It could be an SAP consultant, a former maintenance manager, an enterprise solution architect, or a Primavera consultant. Or it may be somebody who had some previous exposure to a SAP-Primavera integration project, whether with the same toolset or not.

In almost all cases it is a person with senior level experience in a related area. This is as close to an "EPC consultant" as it is likely to get. And not surprisingly, since such a role does not really exist, there is the potential for conflict.

My argument is simple. Almost any advisor only had partial exposure to the full technical and functional scope tackled by the project. While that was helpful during early exploratory stages, the closer it gets to the implementation, the more the outside expert team is likely to take over.

A single person is highly improbable to be completely up-to-date and know all the ins and outs of the various technical and functional solution components. Therefore, while such a person can perform a great role, there are some areas of potential conflict.

My recommendation is to clearly specify the role of this individual through the implementation. Address the conflict, and force its resolution as early as possible. It may totally depend on the individual personality and on priorities of that advisor and of the client. To the implementation team such a person can be an invaluable asset. Everybody just needs to be comfortable with their roles and position.

Vendor Competition

"I need a Citrix connection so that I can access one server."

"Okay, let's have an exploratory phone call, and then we will need to work on a formal Statement of Work. Expect about a week for us to come up with a proper quote."

Have you ever encountered a situation like that? Where a request for seemingly 30 to 45 minutes of effort was turned into a mini-project involving multiple resources, a work effort exceeding 40 hours, and a targeted duration for the delivery of about one month.

I have. And I needed the Citrix connection within 24 hours.

Vendor engagement models can be a serious source of frustration when one just wants to get the job done. I don't want to blame anybody here, just describe situations that will need to be considered. They come in many variations:

- "Hardware support is not managed by this company, but by that one."
- "You want me to adjust your authorization profile? Such a request requires a 3 week lead time - we are totally swamped."

- "You cannot use your own environment, but ours, whether our systems are up or not. Why? Because other people use our systems also."

Whether one likes the above (who would?) or not, one needs to be prepared to deal with it. Many organizations have no less than a dozen or more IT service providers. To not let this turn into a showstopper, this needs to be addressed right away. I see it as one of a project manager's most important roles, to address these issues right away.

Engagement models need to be aligned, support for the project needs to be ensured, and performance and delivery is key. This is, by the way, a main reason why I prefer an internal project manager. There can be a big difference whether a customer calls or a supplier.

This can at times get even more complicated when some of the vendors are actually or potentially competing with each other.

There are many players in the IT world. Most large service organizations are able to offer a wide variety of services, reaching anywhere from hardware support and infrastructure as a service, general technical support, application management, to implementation services, and beyond and in between. On top of that are even many more small niche service providers.

Such competition may at times lead to increased efficiencies, or to inefficiencies if vendors are supposed to play nicely with each other. It just does not always work.

My advice is to be aware of such complexities and integrate them into the Statement of Work for the outside expert team. This can be done openly. Anybody who has been around in IT and in large companies should understand the impact of complexity.

It also is a major risk for the schedule. Addressing it heads-on does therefore mean that the interests of the SAP-Primavera experts should in principle be aligned with the customer's.

Boots on the Ground – or in the Air?

Here is a word about remote work versus onsite work. Find the right mix. There are situations where onsite is indispensable, and situations where onsite reduces productivity.

The SAP-Primavera team I have been working with for many years is distributed around the globe. This makes onsite work not appealing logistically, and we have to rely heavily on providing services remotely.

This has some tremendous benefits:

1. We can work around the clock.

A prime example was the testing phase at a major engineering company in England. During the day the client team, supported by a couple of consultants from Capgemini, walked through their test scripts. In the evening there was a coordination call communicating any issues to Auckland. And in the next morning all issues were addressed, and usually they were resolved.

Another one is when we delivered an integration solution in Cape Town, South Africa. We had a few people on site, testing, working during the day, and discovering and analyzing issues as we went along. Those were sent to the development center in Auckland, New Zealand. By the time we returned on site the next morning, usually all issues had been addressed and resolved!

2. Remote work productivity can be much higher.

There are fewer meetings disturbing thought processes during remote development. The environment is more conducive to being productive for analytical or development tasks - while other team members are still just a Skype call away.

We can work literally around the clock when leveraging different time zones, if necessary also during weekends and holidays. That is more difficult if weekends and holidays are spent traveling. - And no, we don't particularly enjoy working on such days, we just do it if it is necessary to get a job done.

3. Until late in the stage, we can leverage our own development environment.

Yes, sometimes we need to reconfigure SAP ECC or set up some more representative data, to more closely reflect a client's environment. Even that can be an advantage. Such configuration and setup usually can be done quickly if using experienced people. Doing so additionally can help digesting more properly specifications and requirements, leading to more meaningful development work.

4. Remote work can be less expensive.

Only part of that is due to lower travel expenses, although those benefits add up also. Mainly it is due to higher productivity and the ability to work part-time if required. We can organize our workday more flexibly and do not need to hang around as paid consultants because we happen to be at a client's site.

In general I prefer our boots on the ground, and not in the air. That is, for the other guys. I am often living in an airplane and stop by on the ground just to be able to check how far my mileage balance has risen.

5.

WHAT? DESIGN THE RIGHT SOLUTION

The Solution Design Context

"You consultants are just here to rip us off. You are talking and changing everything. Then you leave us with some crap that runs our business right into the ground, while you take our money and continue on to your next gig."

I am paraphrasing here, but the above is as literal a quote as I remember, from one business user during a solution design meeting. Disdain, venom.

And of course unjustified. Yes, of course. Because of course I do not say this like American voters commenting on Congress on the one side (the "others"), and their Representative to Congress on the other ("me"). The first one they hate and give a 10% approval rating, the second one they like and give a 60% approval rating.

Just like me, I am great; it is the other guys who are messing up my reputation.

It is not quite like that. Almost every professional I work with, customer and consultant alike, operates ethically. But there is a lot of half-knowledge around, and many half-truths. How to design and implement integrated solutions is just one of them.

There is a mapping spreadsheet and a PowerPoint slide. And yes, I hear you. You know what you want, you have figured it out, and you really do not understand why it would take another six to eight weeks to have all specifications designed. I have a short answer, which is a fairly long sentence in itself: You have not thought of everything, unless you did a POC and a Prototype and performed multiple rounds of walk-throughs of the project life-cycle coming from different perspectives, and quite likely unless you developed or reviewed your design with experienced technical and functional consultants.

So please follow me through the next pages and see why I consider SAP-Primavera integration to be one of the most complex business solutions out there. It may be my (lack of) intellect or maybe I am getting old, although I still get the occasional "young man" from retirees. Most likely, though, the reason why you think it is quite simple and I think it is very complex is quite logical and not a contradiction.

It has something to do with each portion of the whole being straightforward, but the complete technical, functional, and process picture having dozens and even hundreds of what I like to call "moving parts". It's a classical case of what network theory calls complexity.

The below is just an overview, I am not really going into all the details...

The Functional Solution Design Process

Solution Design Overview

"We know what we want" is not an unusual statement I hear from you when we have our first conversations. That statement soon is being qualified and something to the effect of "basically" or "in principle" is added. If we get beyond that point we discover that the "know" is essentially limited to the basic process and a list of most fields to be transferred.

The solution design did not yet go into details of logical conditions, or describe how the project life cycle impacts the status, or what kinds of errors are to be caught and how they should be revealed, and a myriad of other little details.

On top of that, the implication of technical aspects has not been considered much in the design.

What we usually have is a generic vision of a solution, under consideration of some or most the specific organizational and process context. Not more and not less. And this is exactly where one should be at this stage of the process. As long as there is no misperception about that, we are in pretty decent shape.

I call this "high-level scope", while sometimes people use the term "Scope" or "Blueprint" or "High-level Design". The exact term is not that important, even though in this book I will continue referring to it as high-level scope.

The science and art of designing the complete solution, and to turn this into detailed design specification, is what Step 5 is about.

A Funnel. The solution design process is a funnel. It is based on the high-level scope outlined in a Project Charter or Statement of Work. This scope is validated in a formal workshop, considering a demo or mockup of the envisioned solution and the technical solution landscape.

That validated scope is to be refined in a couple of detailed design workshops. The purpose of the detailed design effort is to provide a comprehensive definition of field-level mappings in line with the overall scope, including all logical conditions to be considered during the implementation.

Proven ways of getting to the final detailed design are to start with a detailed design workshop while using a solution demo and mockup in SAP and Primavera. Subsequently, this first draft of the detailed solution design is reflected in a generic working prototype. That prototype will be reviewed hands-on in a second and final detailed design workshop.

It has shown to be very effective to be able to review detailed design decisions using a prototype that demonstrates the object-level process flow "in principle", including a majority of the detailed mappings. The theoretically designed solution becomes tangible, which gives a new perspective and helps flushing out additional details.

The final detailed design mappings and related logic are reflected in the "build" version of solution, which subsequently is unit tested, integration tested, user acceptance tested, performance tested, authorization tested, and regression tested. Up to right before the Go Live, though, the project team should be open to some detailed design adjustments.

I have never seen a solution that had not at least a few minor adjustments made based on input from various test cycles. That is a good thing, since such changes are usually triggered by reality, and by end-users.

Input: Design Considerations. The following is a list of inputs to be considered during the designing of a specific solution. It is a process of gradual refinement as more of the below will be considered in subsequent reviews of specifications and deliverables.

- Process Description
- Functional Requirements
- Technical Requirements & Landscape
- Solution Mockup or Demo
- Project Life Cycle (scope, cost, time, resources)
- Reporting and Action Requirements
- Real-Life Data
- Business & Test Scenarios

Output: Deliverables. During the solution design process, the following deliverables help documenting progress on specifications. They are working deliverables in the sense that they are refined going forward. The documents will also get more detailed throughout the test cycles. They reflect all input, including last-minute input and fixes discovered and agreed on.

This turns them into an integral part of functional documentation, training, and input for support staff.

- Object-Level Mappings (Document)
- Field-Level Mappings (Document)
- Technical Landscape Diagram (Document)
- Solution Mock-up (System)
- Prototype (System)

Activities. Here is a list of the main formal activities conducted to develop the final solution design. The process is in principle simple. It takes the design considerations as input and produces the deliverables as output.

- Scope Validation Workshop
- Detailed Design Workshop
- Prototype
- Detailed Design Validation Workshop and Prototype Review
- Design Review Calls and Meetings

The Proof of Concept (POC)

Above I challenged the attempt to perform a Proof of Concept (POC) during the tool selection process as being misguided for that purpose. It is a totally different story when the goal of a POC is to help clarifying key design decisions. For that it can add very good value.

Whenever you have the chance to look at an application or even to play around or work with a system as close as possible to the envisioned design, do it. The truth is in the system, and theory can only go so far before it needs to be validated in a tangible manner.

At two good times a POC can make most sense.

One is right before a formal implementation project is started. This is the time to finalize high-level design and to generate more positive excitement about integration really being achieved. At such a time the most useful approach is a "conference room pilot", implying a mockup using a standalone or external environment. By doing so you can cut out architectural and infrastructure issues, like servers not being available or an installation learning curve. It also speeds up the POC development, and you have more options to leverage and incorporate enhancements or add-ons.

The other one is right after the project has been approved, as a formal part of the initial scope validation process. In that context it can become the precursor of a more detailed prototype, playing a similar function. At that time, the POC could include an installation onsite. Pursue this with caution, though, since infrastructure logistics may prove so challenging that it can hold up processes quite a bit.

The scope of most POCs is primarily focused on functionality. While some technical aspects will of course need to be addressed, like installations or the basic flow of information or some logic aspects, usually it stays at that.

Design Workshops

Apart from the initial rounds of testing, design workshops are the most customer-facing parts of the project. They are the main tool to achieve alignment of expectations and technical and functional specifications. Broad participation, not skills is needed to achieve these outcomes.

So what do I mean when I say "workshop"?

In principle it is the getting together and working together of the whole core project team, at times with breakout sessions, to address key challenges that may require expertise from a variety of sources.

Main Sessions. In design or design review sessions you will typically require the whole project team to be present. At times individual members may be excused, and you may identify topics for breakout sessions like issues related to the technical architecture. In general, though, at least the initial part and the conclusion should involve everybody.

"Everybody" in this context includes but may not be limited to all internal and external core team members, covering technical and functional expertise, for SAP, Primavera and of course as main contributors the business team.

Workshops will consist of individual sessions, alternating between joint sessions and individual clarifications. Make sure that each workshop has a clear purpose to produce tangible deliverables. Examples for such deliverables are an object-level mapping diagram, a depiction of the general process flow, a detailed mapping spreadsheet, or a list of business scenarios.

Often many participants need to travel. This will allow them to focus on the agenda and contribute while working together for several days in a row. Keep in mind that you should reserve some time to formally document findings and decisions or decision options. Time may also be needed to research and analyze specific questions. This lends itself to introduce multi-hour breakout sessions during afternoons or mornings.

Workshops are most effective if conducted as a series of consecutive sessions within one week. Their overall duration may be anywhere between two and five days. Typically a high-level scope validation workshop may also involve stakeholders who are able to only contribute more limited time than core team members. Such a workshop will tend to be somewhat shorter, while detailed design sessions more often tend to take a full week.

Consider that workshops will require access to demo systems and to real and representative data.

Breakout and Follow-up Sessions. Not everybody's full attention is required all the time during workshops. Definitely initial overviews, demos and any kind of summary statements should be attended by everybody. I also recommend to have all team members participate at each day of a workshop at least for several hours.

Beyond that time, breakout sessions can be used to keep participants focused on aspects that they can best contribute to. Examples are the analysis of versions of technical solution components, an evaluation of status behavior in SAP, or reporting requirements in Primavera.

Overall process aspects need to be verified by the whole team, and the results of detailed research or analyses should be presented to the whole team. Draft output and final deliverables are to be circulated among all core team members.

Once workshops are completed they should already have a good draft of the core deliverables. Rarely will those be final yet, and additional input may be required, decisions made, or formal aspects considered. If necessary, follow-up sessions will be identified to conclude such open items and finalize the deliverables. Such follow-up sessions may be attended by a subset of the core team.

Object-Level Mappings

An object level mapping describes how two objects in SAP and Primavera relate to each other. These mappings are not yet concerned with detailed fields, which will be listed below each such relationship at a later point in time. Each direction of the relationship has to be treated separately. For example, if high-level WBS elements are created in SAP and then transferred to become Primavera WBS elements, and lower level WBS elements are created in Primavera and transferred to become SAP WBS elements, these will be treated as two separate object relationships.

EPC has the ability to map any two objects. Often it is very straightforward to determine what objects relate to each other, e.g. in the case logical relationships between activities. Others vary widely, particularly those relating to project structures.

Examples for structure-level mappings that are not always straightforward are:

- SAP Project Definition —> Primavera Project
- SAP Revision —> Primavera Project
- SAP WBS —> Primavera Project
- SAP WBS —> Primavera WBS
- Primavera WBS —> SAP WBS
- SAP Activity —> Primavera WBS
- SAP Activity —> Primavera Activity
- Primavera Activity —> SAP Activity

- Primavera Resource Assignment —> SAP Activity

All object-level mappings together cover the basic project flow. They can be used to determine the basic workflows and logical steps according to which the integration will be set up in XSLT.

Detailed Design

The simplest way to think about the detailed design is in the form of field-based specifications in a mapping spreadsheet. This is the most critical piece of output, and a deliverable that becomes the guideline for all delivery of functionality. To develop a detailed design field-level mapping spreadsheet an object-level mapping needs to be in place first.

Detailed mappings break down each of the object-level mappings into their detailed fields and related logic. These can then be validated through various project life cycle review processes. It is helpful to label each field-based mapping so that it can be referred to in code and makes support more straightforward.

Even before you define or refine all logic, use the list of mappings to validate API capabilities. Do that early on since deficiencies, like fields not yet supported by the SAP or Primavera API, will introduce additional research, development and testing effort. That can affect the project timeline. Detailed field-level mappings also provide the basis for the development of unit test scenarios and a checklist for their validation.

Project Life-Cycle – 6 Perspectives

A look at fields can only tell you half the story, if even that. Mapping related fields is necessary for an integration solution, but the real job is to figure out the logic that needs to apply to reflect a real process. As the word implies, something is moving, which means changing, and in project management this is called the project life-cycle.

Throughout the project life cycle, conditions change, and the relationship between specific fields and objects in SAP and

Primavera will be impacted. One activity will get started, another even finished, while a third one is not even completely planned yet. Relationships may be transferred from SAP initially, but then Primavera may take over.

A high-level WBS may be created in SAP, but the lower levels may need to be set up in Primavera. Resources may be associated in Primavera, but budgets may not be available.

All these situations, and the potentially different treatment of the same field-level or even object-level mapping, may exist at the same time. Transfers need to consider this, and doing so is not trivial.

Most of these situations have in common that either the ownership of an object transfers from SAP to Primavera or the other way around, or that the control over what can be done or cannot be done to an object is determined by one or the other application, or an interaction of both.

You may want to walk through the life-cycle up to six times, looking at it from a different perspective each time.

1. *Creating and updating of objects.* Walking through the life cycle, check for each type of objects the directions mappings go, while keeping in mind that they may go both ways based on certain conditions. Look for the specific triggers for selections and create or update transaction. Such triggers may be certain fields (e.g. profit center or functional location fields), portion of the ID (e.g. "the last two characters of the revision field"), or statuses (e.g. a certain user status, or a system status).

2. *Creating and updating of fields.* Walking through the life cycle, check for each field whether it should be updated and overwritten each time, or only created and then not updated anymore, or only updated because it has originally been created manually or in the other application.

3. *Starting, Progressing and Completing of Work.* Again walking through the life cycle, review the status interaction between SAP and Primavera. For example, keep in mind that one can receive a material in SAP and post an actual as soon as it is released, independent on whether it has been started or not. This goods receipt transaction will then create an actual date. Should this activity in Primavera not have started yet, SAP just impacted the Schedule! Consider such interactions on the project level, and for the WBS and Activities, and for the start and finish status of each of these objects.

4. Cost, Date, Time and Resources Management. Walk through the project life cycle with a view on the interactive management of costs, dates and time, and resources. While doing so, review data required for earned value analysis. For example, keep in mind that while dates are to be scheduled in Primavera, certain constraints or guiding dates may be handed down from SAP.

5. Reference Fields. Sometimes one application may have taken ownership of the date while the other one still may have helpful input to offer. One example is the delivery date of a PO, which may be driven from Primavera, even though SAP may suggest a different date.

6. Typical Error Conditions. Walk through the resulting mapping spreadsheet and review for typical errors or conditions you would like to be informed about.

Some Statuses to Consider. A few more words on status management, which can be complex. Unlike Primavera, SAP has a high number of statuses, and they directly affect what one can do in the ERP environment or not. The setting of statuses also can be dependent on certain user authorizations. This requires a careful thinking through each process step.

"Ownership" of a specific instance of an object may in theory be dependent on the other application. E.g., you may want to say in Primavera that an activity has started, but that does not mean much in SAP if a system or user status still prevents postings of actual hours or the receiving of goods for that activity. You may be able to resolve this by having the change of a status in Primavera trigger a status change in SAP.

It may have to be more complex than that, though. I have seen the need to use User-defined Fields (UDFs) or Activity Codes in Primavera to trigger specific statuses. There is a tradeoff to be made here: It adds steps to scheduler's work for reasons that are related to SAP and back-end integration. This may not be intuitive and will require specific attention during documentation and training.

Following is a short and selective list with examples of frequently used statuses. I use generic terms, describing functions of statuses. They may be named or configured differently.

- Ready to be Scheduled.
  A user-defined status that determines whether a planning effort in SAP has been concluded and an operation or activity is ready to be transferred to and "owned" by Primavera.
- Planning Complete.
  A criterion set in Primavera to determine whether a newly created WBS or Activity is ready to be transferred to SAP.
- Scheduled.
  A user-defined status "scheduled" may be used as a criterion to determine whether an activity is ready to be included when sending data back to SAP (e.g. dates).
- Released.
  A SAP system status "released" is used to determine whether an activity can be worked on and whether actuals can be charged to it. If an object was created in Primavera, this status may be triggered by Primavera.
- Technically Complete.
  A SAP status that determines whether all work on an activity or WBS is done. This is different from "complete" since actual posting are still allowed to consider time-delayed reporting of work.
- Progress.
  Also consider the interaction between % completion (progress, POC) and status (see a few more details below in the paragraphs about "Progress").

SAP and Primavera Design

The Design of SAP and Primavera processes can affect how the integration can work. Pay therefore specific attention to any kind of customization or unusual configuration effort, or set up decisions in either one of these applications.

SAP Design. In theory there can be many dozens or even hundreds of configuration and setup aspects to consider. Here are some of the more obvious ones:

- Project ID Masks
- User Statuses
- User Exits
- Custom Fields
- Custom Programming
- Changes to Key Configuration Entries (like control keys or order types)
- Industry-specific Extensions (e.g. linear assets)
- Material Groups
- Authorization

Primavera Design. The following Primavera setup and design aspects may impact the logic to be reflected in the detailed design. At a minimum, set up good test data to simulate cross-application processes. This will help flushing out potential implications on generic mappings.

- Authorizations and related EPS structures
- Scheduling Parameters
- Calendars
- Code Structures and Standards
- Cost Accounts
- ID and Key Structures and Fields
- Multi-Level Linked Projects

The Prototype

The final step before formally starting the Build phase of a SAP-Primavera integration project is to deliver a prototype. Of course this is a bit more already, since in reality a prototype should be decent enough to already be the beginning of the Build phase. It is a rough version of the core mappings, reflecting some key scenarios.

Prototypes will fall short of the final product in several ways:

- Not all fields will need to be mapped.
- Not all logical conditions for field mappings do need to be considered.
- Not all status changes and logical conditions for a complete project life cycle need to be considered.
- Custom error messages will not be addressed (all) yet.
- Performance will not be addressed (fully) yet.
- Some master data may need to be set up manually.
- Authorizations will not yet be considered.

However, prototypes should provide for the ability of a somewhat simplified walk through a full generic process flow. This includes the largest part, or even overwhelming portion, of all mappings, conditional updates, and if possible already the generic user interface to be used.

Although a prototype may be installed on site, I usually don't see a big value-add in that. Most efficient is the rapid-development of the prototype in a development environment, most likely in a remote one provided by the implementing team. That way there are no dependencies on infrastructure, system access, tool installation, or the like.

The purpose is to play back to the business what looks like a close approximation of the final product. This gives the project team a "final" opportunity to validate specifications and to discover logical inconsistencies, missing mappings or logic, special cases, or flaws in the thinking. From that point on this is about finalizing and "tweaking", not about designing anymore.

The prototype should include a representative data sample, and should include a generic running of end-user transactions in SAP and Primavera (e.g. time reports, resource assignments), and reports and layouts that give a meaningful flavor of the overall look and feel of the solution.

A prototype should be formally documented, in enough detail down to the specific use of individual field entries, so that it can be repeated during multiple demos, by the business and not just by consultants.

Key Functional Solution Components

In this section I give a general overview of critical aspects relating to key objects and functional solution components. It is impossible to address all variations and implications, or to make specific recommendations for your business. Much of this depends on the individual context that one finds in each organization.

The art and science of solution design is to be aware of all options, consider all implications, and orchestrate the overall solution in a way that issues are minimized, usability is maximized, and the overall process is supported in the best possible way.

The Project

At a first view it looks so simple: "A project is a project, so what is the question?"

Then it is not so much anymore. In EPC one can map any object to any other object. Often that means that a Primavera Project is not the same as a SAP Project Definition. Here are some examples, slightly simplified, for the context of outage management solutions:

SAP Project Definition ID = Primavera Project ID. I have seen this mapping at two Engineering & Construction companies, one in the Philippines, the other one in Australia.

SAP WBS ID = Primavera Project ID. I have seen this mapping at an outage management solution for an Australian utility, and an owner-based capital project management solution at a Canadian oil company. When using SAP WBS IDs, more conditions need to be applied since in all likelihood not each SAP WBS element is supposed to become its own Primavera project.

SAP Revision ID = Primavera Project ID. I have seen this mapping at a utility in South Africa.

SAP Functional Location ID = Primavera Project ID. This mapping at an American utility was in reality a bit more complex, but the principle is as described.

Primavera Master Schedule WBS ID = Primavera Detailed Schedule Project ID. Here I refer to a mapping that creates a Primavera project based on an object and related setting from another Primavera project. Complex and multi-level project structures may require complex solutions.

Some project-level mappings point out a shortcoming when using the out-of-the-box EPC transaction: It allows for the possibility of missing orders. How would one find out whether a project, consisting of all orders associated with a revision, had an order removed? How can one ensure that projects based on SAP revisions are up to date, even if one has used partial transfers only?

This is a case where an add-on transaction can become valuable, and where custom error messages and logic can help improve data integrity and the completeness of transaction results.

The Work-Breakdown-Structure (WBS)

The practical use of a work breakdown structure in Primavera is much more simple than in SAP, and definitely different.

Concepts. A frequent point of contention is whether the SAP WBS is purely a Cost Breakdown Structure (CBS) and not a WBS. This is a somewhat simplified view and artificial issue. A core function of a WBS in SAP, and in formal project management theory, is to provide more detailed cost and budget-level controls, which means it also is part of a CBS. This breakdown typically reflects core deliverables of work, either by assets or asset group (i.e. in capital projects) or sales order line item (i.e. for sales-related projects). In such a context I cannot detect a conflict between what is seen as primarily a CBS and a WBS.

The SAP WBS can also be used for cost planning, high-level date planning and high-level resource planning. It therefore performs the duplicate function of a WBS and a CBS.

In Primavera the WBS has much more limited capabilities. Most if not all relevant functionality could also be performed by using activity codes to group and sort individual activities. For the interface, one of the most relevant considerations of the Primavera WBS is the automated rolling up of summary data from associated activities.

Following is a list of important mapping consideration related to the Work-Breakdown-Structure.

Mapping Considerations.

- One Typical Flow.
  A typical flow is that the high-level WBS is defined in SAP, reflecting primarily the CBS. More detailed WBS elements are then added in Primavera (or in SAP). These may or may not flow back into SAP (or Primavera).
- WBS IDs.
  These are handled differently in Primavera than in SAP. In SAP each WBS is a unique ID, while in Primavera many WBS IDs can be duplicates (e.g. the number "1" or "2" are likely to be used many times over), as long as they are on a different level. Levels are separated through dots. Primavera displays the inherited parent IDs together with the individual WBS ID.
  SAP IDs are freeform unless limited through a mask. Separators are not limited to dots but could be a range of special characters. Levels are indicated through a level indicator and hierarchies are defined as relationships and not using IDs. Having that said, specific structures of IDs can be used to reflect hierarchies.
- Duplicate WBS Names in Primavera.
  Duplicate names of WBS elements are not allowed in Primavera, while that is no problem with SAP.
- SAP WBS = Primavera WBS.
  This may be the simplest mapping, a 1:1 between SAP and Primavera.

- SAP WBS = Primavera Project.
  Based on some logical trigger, certain SAP WBS elements may result in the creation of their own Primavera project.
- SAP Network = Primavera WBS.
  Primavera has no equivalent to the concept of a network, or network header. Should an equivalent grouping of activities be required, one option is to reflect SAP networks as Primavera WBS elements, or as WBS summary activities together with WBS elements.
- SAP Work Order = Primavera WBS.
  Primavera has no equivalent to the concept of a work order, or work order header. Should an equivalent grouping of activities be required, one option is to reflect SAP work orders as Primavera WBS elements, or as WBS summary activities together with WBS elements.
- SAP Activity = Primavera WBS.
  When interpreting SAP activities as summary activities, they may be best reflected as WBS elements in Primavera.

Activities

Here I use the term "activity" from the Primavera perspective. Depending on the module in SAP, an activity in the PS module is equivalent to an operation in the PM module.

Concepts. Theoretically and conceptually activities or operations in SAP, and activities in Primavera are much alike. They reflect the work effort to be performed to deliver a WBS and eventually the whole project deliverable. In either application they may be linked using relationship logic, and so perform the basis of scheduling calculations.

Overall they are the core objects used to describe what commonly is understood to be a "schedule".

SAP differentiates between four kinds of activities: internal activities, primary cost activities, external activities and service activities. Internal activities assume work delivered by internally managed resources. Examples are "20 Hours of Electrician time", or "6 Hours of Java Development time".

Primary cost activities are used to plan or collect actual costs as lump sums, grouped by a "cost element", the equivalent of an "expense account". Examples would be $200 of "Material Expenses", "Office Materials", or "Travel Expenses - Hotels".

External activities relate to items purchased through the SAP MM module, in almost all cases materials. They may trigger the creation of purchase requisitions and purchase orders, therefore leading to commitments occurring at projects.

External services also relate to items purchased externally, but as the name implies these are external services. The process of purchasing and receiving services differs from the one related to materials.

Primavera differentiates activities mostly by their type of Task Dependent, Resource Dependent, WBS Summary, or Level of Effort (LOE) activity. The first one I see most often used as a "default activity". The latter two can be used to summarize dates from more detailed activities.

Primavera expresses milestones as their own activity type, as either a Start Milestone or a Finish Milestone Activity. In comparison, in SAP these are separate objects.

Mapping Considerations.

- SAP activities may also contain components or production resources and tools (PRTs) that may need to be mapped to Primavera activities also. Components may be delivered to activities based on the activity schedule and according to calculations performed in SAP MRP (materials requirements planning). This means that they may come from the outside or from a warehouse.
- SAP Control Key-based logical conditions may need to be introduced to consider the kind of activity.
- Integration into procurement may require additional data to be pulled for external activities or service activities (e.g. delivery dates, vendors number and vendor name).

- Procurement of long lead material items may be reflected as separate activities or as the assignment of non-labor resources in SAP.
- Consider the interaction between statuses in SAP and Primavera, and the challenges in mapping these throughout the full project life cycle. You can find more information about that above, in the section about the project life cycle.

Milestones

Concepts. Primavera milestones are activities, and can either be Start Milestones or Finish Milestones. In SAP they are separate objects that are either related to activities or to WBS elements. They have a usage and may be used for earned value calculations or to link project progress to billing and revenues.

SAP milestones may therefore also introduce aspects that are not relevant for the more narrow focus of scheduling in Primavera. This turns some SAP milestones into references only, while Primavera milestones may not need to be transferred to SAP for a similar reason.

Mapping Considerations.

- Since SAP milestones can have more functions, be sure you know what exactly you want to use them for. For example, you may use milestones to indicate relationships with billing schedules, or to perform earned value analysis.
- When creating SAP milestones from Primavera, consider additional details and defaults, like how to map types of milestones, and what function they are supposed to perform in SAP.
- Consider whether there is a real need to transfer milestones, and how to filter relevant milestones from informative milestones or those that are not relevant for the respective other application.

Relationships

This is a straightforward mapping, and not used too frequently. The concepts of relationships are very similar between SAP and Primavera. In both cases one can define logical links between two activities as Finish-Start (FS), Start-Start (SS), Start-Finish (SF) or Finish-Finish (FF).

One potential complexity may creep into mappings because lag may be expressed using different units of time. Since relationships rarely are transferred, and if then usually without lag or overlap, this rarely is a real issue.

Relationships are an intricate part of a schedule, and you may change them frequently in Primavera. Therefore they should also be owned by Primavera. However, sometimes relationships are established and stored in SAP as reference data. This is typically the case in respect to maintenance tasks, where relationships are stored as task lists. With planning of maintenance operations usually performed in SAP, the initial download of operations into Primavera activities may include relationships.

Uploads of final versions of a schedule into SAP may function as references for the future are more tricky to do. Such an upload would need to tackle reference structures like task lists, and that can be a one-to-many relationship. I have only seen one client do that, in a limited manner.

Resources

Concepts. Primavera has three kinds of resources, labor, non-labor and materials. These resources can have codes or user-defined fields associated with them. Sometimes additional roles structures are used. Nevertheless, for labor the resource library does not nearly have meaningful human resources functionality. Qualifications, certifications, individualized calendars and matrix-type management structures cannot be reflected.

Similarly, materials or non-labor resources do not even touch the surface of materials or resource management capabilities of a full-fledged ERP application. Primavera has no concept of logistics, stock, or procurement, all of which are core capabilities of SAP. That means that decisions need to be made about to what degree the ERP complexity should be reflected in Primavera.

The answer is rarely to load "everything" into Primavera. Rather I recommend to do it on a "need-to-know" basis. If there are date limitations coming out of SAP procurement activities, send them to Primavera (and vice versa). If certifications of individual resources are a decision criterion for whether a person should be assigned to an activity or not, you may consider pulling that information from SAP.

However, in most cases I have observed information about individual resources or about each individual material purchased cannot reasonably well be integrated into a schedule, and definitely such a schedule cannot be managed effectively.

Although SAP labor or material resources can be managed in a much more complex manner, the reality is that most of that information may not be relevant in real-life. At some level one needs to assume that team leaders or gang leaders, or whatever the respective manager's label is, know enough or even more about their people anyway. They are then the ones who will make this decision, not a software application or a somewhat more removed scheduler or planner.

SAP also has a solution called "multi-resource scheduling" that in theory allows complex scheduling and supports the assignment of resources using detailed human resources data. In theory this is a very powerful instrument, but there are logical and practical limitations. This is a more philosophical and strategic question, though, since MRS' effective use does almost completely preclude the use of Primavera. For the purposes of this book we assume that the decision has been made to use an external scheduling system, i.e. Primavera.

Mapping Considerations.

- The behavior of the out-of-the-box sample delivered by SAP is that a work center resource will be created during the transfer if it is discovered that it has been assigned to a project activity or operation, and if this resource does not exist in Primavera. This may not be sufficient, particularly if resources are to be assigned, or assignments are to be changed, in Primavera.

- Work centers in SAP are plant-specific. Primavera resources will therefore need a prefix of the SAP plant code. For a similar reason typically the SAP plants will become a top-level hierarchy in the Primavera resources library. Sometimes it may be helpful to add one more hierarchy node, like one based on SAP usage or capacity type. This would not reflect SAP resource hierarchies, but a grouping in Primavera according to an SAP setting.

- When resource assignments are to be made in Primavera, this means that each time any data is transferred the resource library is to be updated. If not, this could lead to data inconsistencies.

- Decide what to do with work center hierarchies. Those can be reflected in Primavera, but only if the complete libraries are synchronized, not just individual resources that are assigned in SAP. Such hierarchies will then need to be updated after creation, to prevent them getting out of sync.

- Although materials are formally resources in SAP, selecting those that are relevant for the schedule can be very tricky. Therefore, they are usually not mapped unless associated with a specifically set up external activity. I have seen a customer mapping materials to resources, but that led to such an overload of small materials being transferred that this mapping was stopped.

- SAP work centers and human resources records can have a status. Decide on how to consider that status and whether a change in status in SAP will affect the validity of resource assignments that have been transferred to Primavera.

- Determine to what degree it is important to differentiate in Primavera between internal resources and procured resources, and how this information may need to be pulled from the services procurement modules in SAP.

- Although relevant mostly for internally managed projects that predominantly use internal resources, it may be helpful to pull master records of individual people from SAP into Primavera. All above considerations for work centers apply here also, like statuses, hierarchy changes, and what specific additional data fields to pull.

- Resources can have rates in SAP and in Primavera. However, SAP has much more flexibility, e.g. in the number of rates. Mapping rates and keeping them in sync can turn into a major logical challenge. Therefore consider sticking to the strength of each application, which would leave cost management primarily with SAP, and time management with Primavera.

Resource Assignments

Concepts. The transfer of resource assignments is a step separate from the transfer of resources. The second one synchronizes the resource libraries, while the first one determines which resource is assigned to perform what activity. Here we have a logic issue. Obviously you can only assign a resource that exists in the application that you are assigning it in. This does then imply that at any point of time the assigning application needs to have a complete resource library available.

The default behavior of the EPC sample mappings is to create a new resource in Primavera whenever an assignment is found in SAP. This works as long as the resources are assigned in SAP and not in Primavera. Should the intention be to assign resources in Primavera, then the complete library needs to be synchronized in advance of each assignment.

In SAP, a typical labor resource assignment is expressed as a work center field on an activity or operation. Potentially this work center could be individualized by assigning a specific human resources master record to the activity, as a subset of the work center. Multiple resource assignments are reflected in a duplication of objects. In SAP PS this is done by adding activity elements to an activity, in SAP PM the equivalent object is a sub-operation.

Particularly when assigning resources in Primavera, a main challenge may be the approval of the resources plan. In SAP it would be done through status management, although this is not really considered a very user-friendly feature. Primavera does not have such a capability.

Mapping Considerations. Mapping and transferring resource assignments can affect costs and the schedule on both applications. Desired effects do therefore need to be thought through completely, or even better: prototyped and tested. Here are a few key considerations:

- In Primavera exactly one resource is characterized as a primary resource through an indicator. Determine the logic to make clear which SAP resource should be characterized as such.
- Determine the number of resources assigned to perform an activity, whether this number may be changed in Primavera (as "Units/Time", to allow more control over a schedule's duration), and how that relates back to the schedule. Consider also that different work hours and shifts may have different rates, like overtime rates, and that these rates may only be kept in SAP. An assignment in Primavera may therefore impact costs.
- Should resources be assigned in Primavera, such an assignment may need to be fed back into SAP. This is particularly important if the posting of actual time or cost should be possible, to the specific resource assignment. In SAP a valid activity element and work center or HR master record will need to exist for the CATS or CAT2 transaction, or activity-based allocations of time entries to be performed.
- Primavera resource assignments may have codes and user-defined fields. One of these is used to map each resource assignment to SAP, by adding the SAP activity element ID.
- Ensure process consistency, e.g. by enforcing whether the transfer always should allow work center or HR record assignments from both the activity/operation and the activity element/sub-operation.
  Alternatively, only one or the other may be allowed.
- Consider how the re-assignment of resources should be communicated to the scheduler. Few things bother a scheduler more, and rightly so, than having relevant

scheduling information changed by somebody else or an interface, without effectively informing him or her.

Units

The concept of units in Primavera relates to the quantifiable outcome of an activity. Examples would be cubic yard of concrete poured, or meters of cable laid. This is different from hours worked. The closest SAP comes to that is using Statistical Key Figures, although theoretically activity types could also be used.

I have only rarely found a need to transfer units, although it is worthwhile discussing that topic as part of the long-term strategy to measure progress of service projects. For example, it may not be relevant for the management of turnarounds, but would be very helpful to validate physically observed progress reporting by subcontractors to a general contractor or the owner.

Costs

Question *any* transfer of cost information between SAP and Primavera! This is my simple recommendation. I am not saying that you should never bring cost information across, just that you should question each aspect of it. The reason is that it is impossible to replicate SAP's cost management capabilities in Primavera, which means that whatever is transferred from SAP into Primavera will inevitably be incomplete and therefore not "correct".

Concepts. One of the most basic distinctions between SAP and Primavera is that SAP has a core strength in cost management and Primavera in time management. The closer one stays to this division, the more efficient and streamlined the overall solution will be.

SAP has dozens of ways of planning costs or posting actual costs to project objects like WBS elements or activities. These often have approval steps involved, are status controlled, impact financial statements and cash flow, may involve exchange rates and have tax implications, are integrated into corporate procurement processes, and are part of a corporate-wide budgeting process.

Transferring cost information from SAP with the intention for it to be actively used in Primavera requires a very logically consistent thought process that is implemented as a standardized business processes in a very disciplined manner. This is even more important if the intention is to drive some of the cost planning or budgeting numbers in SAP from Primavera.

Trying to go the other way around, from Primavera to SAP, throws up even more challenges. One would need to compromise the scope of "cost planning" or "budgeting" by excluding material or purchases, allocations and various kinds of overhead, a limited number of resources, and even differences in Primavera concepts of calendars as opposed to the SAP concept of periods.

Mapping Considerations.

- Consider only bringing reference information from SAP into Primavera.
- If possible, stay away from mapping resource-level cost rates. SAP is much more flexible than Primavera regarding that, and this may lead to inconsistencies, and performance implications.
- When planning detailed costs in Primavera, keep the number of accounts as low as possible, and ideally mapped to just a few accounts in SAP (e.g. labor, materials, contractors, other).
- Consider the timing when transferring cost information. If contractor invoices are booked once a month, or time sheet interfaces are only run once a week on Saturday, running transfers on a Wednesday may not allow one to draw good earned value conclusions.

Dates

Concepts. Saying that Primavera should own the schedule essentially means that start and finish dates in SAP are coming from Primavera. It implies that SAP scheduling capabilities are turned off. There is no real need to transfer relationships or durations, since only dates are important.

Despite this seemingly being a straightforward mapping, there are possible complications. Dates may not only update SAP internal activities, but affect the procurement of materials also as a "delivery date". This can also go the other way around, with MRP or procurement or even sales documents introducing constraints or at least providing reference information about realistic delivery or expected completion dates.

You may also make a decision on how project dates and WBS dates and Milestone dates interact between SAP and Primavera. They may become anticipated start and finish dates, or references, or even constraints, providing meaningful information to the scheduler.

Mapping Considerations.

- Set SAP system status DSEX for each activity so that there is not even the possibility for SAP to change and overwrite dates. I recommend a double-firewall approach by using Primavera dates and overwriting SAP constraints also. Therefore, even if somebody were to schedule in SAP after all, Primavera-set constraints would ensure that dates are not affected.
- I do usually not pay attention to durations in SAP. If Primavera calculates the dates, SAP durations are not meaningful no matter how the system derives them, and even if they differ from Primavera durations due to different calendar settings.
- Consider server settings and daylight savings time. These 1-hour differences have at times cost days to analyze and fix.
- Do not try to synchronize calendars. The most would be manually (and "hard") mapping an SAP factory calendar ID to a Primavera calendar ID. However, this would be only to establish a default in Primavera. Since Primavera owns the dates, and has the ability to granularly change working schedules mid-stream, e.g., any attempt to map would in all likelihood not just be meaningless but also very complicated.
- Consider how the posting of actual dates in SAP, or status changes, can affect the Primavera schedule.

Progress

Concepts. Progress reporting is about completion of an activity or WBS element. It is the equivalent of percentage complete, and that is how SAP usually looks at it. Therefore, updates into SAP may trigger a confirmation transaction, although they may also report "POC - percentage of completion" as a condition to be used in SAP earned value calculations.

Progress is typically reported in Primavera as the main execution management tool.

Mapping Considerations.

- Some older versions of the Primavera API do not support rolling up of percent complete from an activity to the WBS.
- Decide where the percent complete will need to be loaded into SAP, either on the activity or on the WBS level.
- Note that there is a tricky relationship between progress and status of an object. For example, if in Primavera a previously 0% completed activity is progressed to 10%, it has to be started. This requires the SAP status to be released to allow posting of actual hours. Likewise, but the other way around, the posting of actual hours in SAP will mean that an activity should be set to started in Primavera.

  Once an activity has been 100% completed in either application, this may also require the setting of a status. However, let's assume you progressed an activity in Primavera to 100%, set it to "Finished" and this would trigger a status update to status CLSD. At that moment SAP would not be able anymore to receive and post invoices, service receipts or CATS or CAT2 transactions that contain actual hours.

  These are just some of the permutations to consider. As I said, it's tricky.
- There may be an approval process and related workflow to be implemented for progress reporting. A standard way of addressing this would be a status or workflow in SAP. It could in theory also be done in Primavera, although almost all options are pure workarounds.

- Consider that progress reporting in a multi-level schedule may be more complex, although more capable, too. Progress may be reported bottom-up, through entries in a Detailed Schedule, and approved in a Master Schedule.

Technical Solution Landscape

Technical Solution Landscape Overview

Most of the technical solution landscape should have been agreed on during the setting of realistic tactical parameters (Step 2, above). Now I will dive deeper into the details of the large number of technical solution components and how they relate to each other architecturally.

The overall technical solution landscape required for the implementation and support of a SAP-Primavera integration solution will look somewhat similar to the below. Please note that the releases and versions of the individual software components are examples only.

SAP publishes a Product Availability Matrix (PAM) document that lists all the software releases and versions that they formally support. However, the PAM only lists formally completed tests and reviews, and is therefore incomplete. In principle all software versions supported by NetWeaver are supported, or in the case of Primavera those databases and Java Application Servers that Oracle publishes from time to time.

I have several times noticed significant challenges in setting up environments when small factors were changed. In recent years there have been less of these cases, and they were typically sorted out faster. It nevertheless is important to keep that in mind when making assumptions and planning and scheduling project activities.

Something as seemingly simple as using a different flavor of UNIX may lead to the need for research and analyses and troubleshooting, possibly taking days or weeks to resolve. If that happens, hopefully the schedule has enough float for that task to prevent it getting on the critical path and pushing out the whole implementation plan.

My list below contains 15 different components, relating to the above graph:

1. SAP ECC
2. Primavera P6 Database
3. SAP EPC ABAP Component
4. NetWeaver Java Application Server (AS)
5. SAP EPC Java Component
6. SAP EPC XSL Files [Samples; including Saxon]
7. SAP EPC Database: SQL
8. Java Development Kit (JDK)
9. WebLogic Java Application Server
10. Primavera P6 API Client
11. Primavera P6 API Server
12. EPC Plus Custom RFCs
13. EPC Plus Custom XSL Files
14. EPC Plus Java-Related Enhancements
15. EPC Plus ABAP-Related Enhancements

You can in theory set up a complete environment in an effort counting hours. However, that is only theoretically possible and with a lot of experience and when not in any way restricted by corporate policies, standards, security, authentication and authorization concerns. The reality is that in our experience it is likely to take a couple of weeks, and sometimes up to a month until everything is stable.

Even after hardware is purchased or provided as virtual servers, there are many little aspects to consider. Hiccups may be introduced when dealing with network access, database passwords, server versions, licenses, authentication and active directory and LDAP, server names, Primavera IDs and passwords, SAP IDs and passwords, etc. These various pieces usually are provided by different departments in an organization, following their own procedures and policies.

Additionally you want to keep documenting installation procedures and do know-how transfer as well as possible. Otherwise you will find a Development environment nicely set up without an understanding of how it was done. Then you need to revisit the whole process when it comes to the setting up of Test and Production environments, still fully dependent on external support.

An Expert's Perspective: The Devil in the Details

"A client had a remotely hosted Primavera environment that needed the Primavera API installed and setup. Due to security requirements, a VPN had to first be established from the client site to the vendor's datacenter and the API servers provisioned by the vendor.

Administrative overhead and approvals delayed the startup for installing the API and of the VPN by more than a month. Coordinating activities across multiple departments and suppliers doubled that time until the setup was complete. Once we were able to establish a connection from SAP to Primavera using the API server, we began experiencing intermittent connection drops. This prompted more than two additional months of troubleshooting and conference calls involving myself, three SAP Basis and networks personnel on the client's side and numerous personnel on the vendor's side. Finally it was determined that the solution was to disable a filtering service.

What should have been a relatively small piece of the puzzle that takes less than 2 minutes to configure in EPC, ended up taking nearly five months to sort out.

For comparison, I have been able to completely setup an internal end-to-end system for CEI, including Primavera, NetWeaver and EPC while sitting in the lobby of a repair shop waiting for my car to be serviced. "

Gregory Richardson
Integration Consultant &
Master of Installations

In theory, all components could be installed on the same server. In reality, however, at least four servers are used, one each for SAP ECC, NetWeaver and the EPC Java Component, the Primavera P6 API, and the Primavera P6 Database.

Software Components in more Detail

How do all these technical architecture pieces fit together and what are some of the main considerations related to each one of them? Let me provide a little more information for each one of the above-mentioned 15 software components.

1. SAP ECC. Usually you do not have to do much here since this is a "given". As long as you have ECC 6 or higher you will be fine. Your Basis team will take care of everything. Every once in a while they will need to tune some database table, set up an authorization or two (i.e. for the EPC connection itself), install the EPC ABAP component, install NetWeaver for the EPC Java component, or help out with Transports. That is it - normally.

2. Primavera P6 Database. This is the Primavera application itself, consisting essentially of the database. Indirectly related with the database, and not explicitly mentioned here, are the Primavera P6 Web Client, used for administrative functions, and the Primavera P6 "Thick" Client. This is usually also a "given", although frequently the implementation of an integration solution is used as a reason to consolidate Primavera databases or to upgrade to a more recent release.

Just in case somebody missed that: We are talking about the client-server product here, not about standalone Primavera P3.

3. SAP EPC ABAP Component. Although the core EPC application is built in Java and installed on a separate NetWeaver server, EPC also requires the installation of an ABAP component. This ABAP piece performs several functions and consists mainly of the out-of-the-box transactions, and logs.

4. NetWeaver Java Application Server (AS). EPC runs on the NetWeaver Java Application Server, previously NetWeaver CE. I strongly recommend to dedicate this application server to EPC, although in theory multiple applications could be run on it at the same time. Sharing NetWeaver with other applications makes maintenance and support more difficult, and complicates development and performance tuning.

The installation of NetWeaver is usually done by a SAP Basis Administrator. Then the NetWeaver Administrator portal is used to manage the "configuration" of EPC, meaning its setting up and connecting to the other applications.

5. SAP EPC Java Component. The EPC Java Component sits on the NetWeaver Java AS. It contains the core EPC code and its EAI application, including the adapters for SAP and Primavera (and MS Project Server), and detailed log files.

6. SAP EPC XSL Files [Sample files; including Saxon]. These files contain all out-of-the-box code used to pull and push, map, transform and transfer data from and to SAP and Primavera. The use of XSL (EXtensible Markup Language) makes this process machine and human readable. XSL transforms data from a "canonical model" to a "local model", and vice versa (Cim2Lim and Lim2Cim). They are installed together with the EPC Java Component.

Note:

Saxon is the officially recommended XSLT processor, and should be installed with the XSL files.

7. SAP EPC Database: SQL. NetWeaver requires a database to be installed. This database stores administrative data and settings, and log files, but no transactional data. EPC supports multiple databases, although in almost all cases I see either MS SQL or Oracle.

8. Java Development Kit (JDK). A Java Development Kit is used by EPC, NetWeaver and Primavera. Be sure to use a version that supports all three of these applications.

9. WebLogic. Either WebLogic or another J2EE-compliant application server is required to host the Primavera API. Since it is an Oracle product like Primavera it often makes most sense to use WebLogic. I have seen few issues only when using other application servers, though.

10. Primavera P6 API Client. The Primavera API Client is to be installed twice, on the same server as the API and on the NetWeaver server.

11. Primavera P6 API Server. The Primavera P6 API Server is to be installed on the JSEE/WebLogic server.

12. EPC Plus Custom BAPIs and RFCs. These are EPC enhancements. They contain API calls from and to SAP ECC, built in ABAP, that replace or enhance the standard BAPIs. All EPC Plus components are built by Competitive Edge International, Inc.

13. EPC Plus Custom XSL Files. These are EPC enhancements or modifications. As I mentioned frequently in this book, the SAP-delivered out-of-the-box XSLT files are samples only and not suited for production use in any complex environment. Custom XSLT files, like those delivered by CEI as advanced templates or components, contain custom workflows and steps and all logic and API calls (including calls to custom BAPIs and RFCs) to tailor the integration to an organization's specific requirements.

Custom XSLT files may also contain some advanced functions, like the CEI conditional updates engine. All EPC Plus components are built by Competitive Edge International, Inc.

14. EPC Plus Java-Related Enhancements. These are EPC enhancements. For example, CEI does at times use custom API calls into the Primavera database, or custom functions for log maintenance. All EPC Plus components are built by Competitive Edge International, Inc.

15. EPC Plus ABAP Add-ons. These are EPC enhancements. For example, CEI provides Add-ons to optimize performance of transfers, add additional transfer controls, transfer simulations, and enhanced error handling. These add-ons interact with the core EPC Java Component and EPC XSLT files. All EPC Plus components are built by Competitive Edge International, Inc.

Additional Technical Solution Components

Following is a short list and summary description of components that address known issues or advanced requirements for typical complex implementations (aren't they all?). These components and their value were already described above (Step 3). For more details, please read up there.

In the below list I refer to products from Competitive Edge International (CEI) that address the respective advanced solution requirements. See www.cei-corp.com.

1. API Enhancements.

Advanced BAPIs cover the basic functionality of standard BAPIs, combine them, and add the ability to interact with a large number of additional data elements ranging, e.g., from the creation of activities in SAP, reading and writing of custom fields in PS or PM, pulling of data from the SAP MM, SD or HR module, or the setting of user or system statuses.

Such enhanced BAPIs offered by CEI contain performance optimization features. All custom BAPIs only become useful if addressed by custom XSLT code.

2. Conditional Updates.

The out-of-the-box XSLT provided by SAP Labs does not contain the ability to realtime compare data between SAP and Primavera and logic based on results of such a comparison of fields or settings. Such update logic may range from simple "overwrite or not" conditions to complex update controls.

CEI offers a conditional updates engine as part of all its XSLT-related solution components, including advanced process templates.

3. Transfer Controls. ("Transfer Manager")

Out-of-the-box EPC as delivered by SAP does not consider the ability for detailed controls of transfers. Additional transfer controls are necessary to give users full control of transfers as required in many real-life scenarios.

Among other capabilities, the CEI Transfer Manager offers transfer controls for starting and stopping transfers, viewing transfer progress and numbers of errors, the reprocessing of errors only, and the ability to dynamically change batch sizes and numbers of threads.

4. Performance Optimizer. ('Transfer Manager')

In my experience, performance of EPC is usually only acceptable for limited scenarios and overall smaller projects. If updates of large data volumes need to be performed daily or even multiple times daily, the solution needs to be re-designed and enhanced through ABAP add-ons that minimize the number of objects to actually being transferred.

CEI's Performance Optimizer is such an ABAP add-on delivered as part of its Transfer Manager.

5. Enhanced Error Handling. ('Synchronization Manager')

The out-of-the-box EPC displays default SAP and Primavera error messages and stores details in error logs. To empower support organizations and even enable user to analyze issues themselves, error messages need to be translated and displayed in more meaningful manner.

CEI's advanced error handling features are delivered as part of its Synchronization Manager.

6. Transfer Simulation. ('Synchronization Manager')

A commonly mentioned feature not available through out-of-the-box EPC is the ability to preview transfer results and perform corrective action of likely errors.

CEI's Synchronization Manager includes the ability to run transfer simulations that do not update the target system but display simulated changes and related error messages.

7. Concurrency Controls. ('Synchronization Manager')

Neither the Primavera API nor EPC offer concurrency controls. This has the potential to lead to data integrity issues.

CEI's Synchronization Manager includes a locking strategy that prevents running more than one transfer to or from the same Primavera Project.

8. User-Friendly Transfer Reports. ('Synchronization Manager')

Schedulers frequently ask for the ability to get an overview of what data changed during a transfer, and what error messages require their attention.

CEI's Synchronization Manager delivers detailed and user-friendly reports of all data changed through transfers.

9. Data Conversion.

The specific sequence of steps performed during SAP-Primavera integration typically assumes the start with a new project. When projects are already in process, special transfers mechanisms need to be applied to make sure that links between SAP and Primavera objects can be established during these one-time conversion events.

CEI offers data conversion tools based on its Synchronization Manager and the ability to use custom transfers that contain specific mapping logic, foreign key relationships, and reports to facilitate the data conversion process. Make no mistake - data conversion can still not fully be automated, and data conversion requirements need to be baked in very early into the mapping and transfers logic, and into the Synchronization Manager.

10. Primavera to Primavera Integration. ('P6 to P6 Transfer')

The Project Management Book of Knowledge (PMBOK), like other advanced industry practices, differentiates between multiple levels of schedules. In a practical business context, these may be reflected as master schedules versus component schedules, contractor schedules, or more generally control account schedules. A standard multi-level schedule solution can be reflected using links between Primavera master schedule and detailed schedules.

CEI's P6 to P6 Transfer enables the linking and synchronization of multiple schedules in one comprehensive solution.

An Expert's Perspective: P6-to-P6 Integration!

"My single biggest discovery about EPC was the realization that EPC is not just capable of transferring data between SAP and P6. At a client we suggested that if EPC could transfer data from SAP to P6 and P6 to SAP then it could just as easily transfer data from P6 to P6. This worked very well and is now part of a standard EPC Plus template that we offer.

I don't think we, or our clients, have yet exploited this capability anything like to its true potential. As well as synchronization within EPC, it could be used for data migration and conversion, especially in combination with SAPs Microsoft Project Adaptor, or with CEI's SQL adaptor we could even bring in data from third party applications. Another potential use is during initiation of large outage projects, where the requirement is to replicate relationships and scheduling information from the previous turnaround while setting up the schedule for the new one."

Angus Scott-Knight
SAP-Primavera Integration Guru

---

11. Resources Transfer.

The EPC out-of-the-box XSLT does not consider processes in which resources are assigned in Primavera.

CEI's "Resources Transfer" consists of API enhancements and custom XSLT that enables the synchronization of complete resource libraries from work centers and associated HR master records, including their hierarchies.

12. Solution Templates.

By reflecting industry-typical practices and processes, and including all applicable additional functional capabilities, advanced process solutions can reduce implementation risks, spread proven good practices, and deliver complete business solutions covering aspects of SAP ECC, Primavera, and of the integration itself. They go far beyond the functional, technical, and process capabilities of the out-of-the-box sample, but integrate them into a complete, powerful solution that ensures high user satisfaction.

CEI's "OMS" - Outage Management Solution is such a template, covering state-of-the-art outage and turnaround management processes. Other solution templates developed address make-to-order, general contractor service delivery, owner-based capital processes, and routine maintenance.

Tailoring Solutions: Workflows, Steps, Mappings

The highest-level configuration entity in EPC is a workflow. In simple terms, a workflow consists of steps, depicting the logical sequence in which the application performs actions. Examples for these are:

> *Request transfer*
> *→ Request project data*
> *→ Restructure WBS*
> *→ Request Primavera data*
> *→ Apply create only rules*
> *→ Structure data in Primavera format*
> *→ Update Primavera and receive response*
> *→ Structure data in SAP format*
> *→ Send Response to SAP*

The sequence of these steps may be different for each implementation, reflecting differences in the business logic to be applied on a generic level. Detailed mappings and their logic are then defined in separate files.

To reflect the business process of an organization, either one of these may be modified:

1. Multiple workflows may be required. For example, one may go from SAP to Primavera, the other one from Primavera to SAP. These are then run in a specified sequence.
2. The steps and their sequence may be different.
3. The specific field-level mappings may differ.
4. The specific logic associated with each mapping may differ.

The above, and the required technical enhancements and add-ons through ABAP, Java or XSLT - this is what solution design is for.

Solution by Process

Outage and Turnaround Management

Business Context. A turnaround is a large-scale periodic maintenance project planned and scheduled up to 24 months in advance. It temporarily takes out of service an entire processing or production unit of an industrial plant ("outage"). Turnaround scope covers essential maintenance, inspection and operations activities to ensure plant safety, performance and reliability that cannot be executed during normal operations.

Turnarounds typically have a long-term planning effort combined with a short-term outage of between 20 to 60 days. The main costs associated with the outages may not be the cost of performing outage activities, but the lost revenues out of the downtime of the facility. This is what makes the integration of the schedule into the maintenance management backend system invaluable. One outage alone can pay for the implementation of the complete integrated solution.

Depending on the industry, the outages themselves may also be more limited and short-term, and more frequent, e.g. for a railroad. A special case of an outage is a nuclear refueling outage, where the outage has an operational trigger for keeping the plant able to produce power. In all these cases the underlying concept as relating to SAP-Primavera integration remains the same, though.

Key Functional Characteristics.

- Selection of scope by revision, including multiple stages
- Separation between project (budget control) and revision (scope control)
- Separation between planning (in SAP) and scheduling (in Primavera)
- Resources controlled by SAP
- Resources and resource assignments loaded from SAP into Primavera
- Relationships from SAP during activity creation
- Limited material interaction (purchased in advance)
- Status controls, i.e. from SAP, and to feed back information to planners
- Change control through SAP (sent to specific Primavera EPS Node to inform schedulers)
- Probable integration of some capital work into the outage context

Options. The following functionality is optional and depends on the specific business processes to be reflected:

- Earned Value, more likely in SAP (due to frequency of updates), but Primavera is also possible
- Focus of Primavera reporting on sign-offs by inspectors
- Activity-code based reporting
- Updating of number of resources used is either done in SAP or in Primavera
- Feeding back of relationships from Primavera into SAP task lists

Recommended or Required Add-ons and Enhancements.

For Turnarounds and Outages, the highest-value challenges to be tackled by add-ons deal with the high data volume and high frequency of updates during the actual outage itself.

- Conditional Updates
- Transfer Controls
- Transfer Performance Optimization
- Missing Order Identification
- Transfer Preview and Simulation
- API Enhancements

Future Functionality. The above describes common and proven solution components for turnaround and outage management. Technology and advanced principles enable the following additional functions and features, which further could enhance the overall value of the solution.

- List of scheduled activities and feedback should be fed directly to individual end users (i.e. through mobile technology)
- Real-time feedback loops from individual users to feed back progress to schedulers, planners, and management (i.e. through mobile technology)
- Earned-value standards that reflect rapid advances of the turnaround, or rather earned-value type reports based on hours rather than costs (schedule is key!)
- Identification of network-type statistics (e.g. number of changes, time between updates and approvals)
- Tightening up of the link between formal budget and cost-related controls and cost plan versions (e.g. through real-time user-based time reporting)

Capital Projects: Owner-Managed

Business Context. Major capital projects have very big budgets, complex procurement processes, and long time lines.

They have two major perspectives: The owner and the general contractor(s). The main concern on the owner's side is to ensure that project progress and risk are managed, and aligned with invoicing. This requires a tight integration into procurement, and finding the right balance for the level of integration into the general contractor's schedules.

In principle the solution is defined by an overall schedule managed by the owner in Primavera, derived from the high-level budgetary and procurement driven structure coming out of SAP. Lower level schedules can be managed by general contractors.

It can be helpful to differentiate between two levels of schedule in the owner's Primavera environment, a program schedule and a master schedule. The program schedule would be aligned with the SAP CBS structure, while the master schedule would link to the general contractors' main project schedules. Alternatively, what I call the program schedule could also directly be mapped to the level of the contractors' main schedules.

In either way, the concept of integrating contractors' main schedules into an owners' schedule means that these processes should be aligned well. - General contractors would likely have lower level schedules also, whose details they may or may not

Key Functional Characteristics.

- Selection of scope through projects or high-level WBS elements
- Division of overall project into large sub-projects
- Relationship between financially controlled cost breakdown structure (CBS) and schedule-driven work breakdown structure (WBS)
- Strong use of general contractors to deliver major sub-projects
- Project progress and earned-value-type reporting requirements
- Resources controlled by contractors, and therefore only a minimum number of internal resources will be in Primavera
- Variations for procurement relationships, but predominantly EPC - engineer, procure, construct
- Physical integration of contractor schedules, or sharing of schedules in one environment

- Contractors may not always use the same scheduling tool (e.g. MS Project or Primavera)
- Before completion of the whole project, some maintenance and operations activities may already commence
- SAP contains high-level structure and budget (e.g. a program schedule, or master schedule)
- Primavera contains general contractor's schedules
- Frequency of updates is smaller than with outages, typically once a week
- Data volume may be big, but performance requirements are more relaxed than comparable turnarounds, due to the lower frequency
- Sign-off processes on progress, including related reconciliation with procurement
- Integration of Primavera schedule with SAP procurement activities for labor and materials
- Integration of Primavera schedule with cash flow management in SAP

Options. The following functionality is optional and depends on the specific business processes to be reflected:

- Sharing of Primavera Master Schedules with general contractors to enable top-down push of project expectations
- Primavera (Program Schedule) to Primavera (Master Schedule) integration
- Variations of progress updates are possible (e.g. units, physical inspection, duration-based)

Recommended or Required Add-ons and Enhancements. For the owner-managed capital projects schedule, the highest-value challenges to be tackled by add-ons deal with the management of the procurement aspects of multi-level schedules, to be clear about progress, reconciliation of with billings, and to determine risks for schedule and cost overruns.

- Conditional Updates
- API Enhancements (i.e. integration into procurement processes)

- Advanced Solution Templates (i.e. split into multi-level schedules)

Depending on the depth of the integration, the data volume of integration may warrant considering additional transfer management capabilities:

- Transfer Controls
- Transfer Performance Optimization
- Transfer Preview and Simulation

Future Functionality. The above describes common and proven solution components for the owner-managed portion of capital projects management. Technology and advanced principles enable the following additional functions and features, which further could enhance the overall value of such a solution.

- List of scheduled activities and feedback should be fed directly to individual end users (i.e. through mobile technology)
- Automated consolidation of contractor schedules into the owner's master schedule

ENC Contractor Service Projects

Business Context. In most cases, complex service projects delivered by general contractors (GCs) are the mirror image of owner-based capital investment projects. The contrasting perspective on the same project results in a number of similarities and differences. Contractors delivering major projects usually need to manage many more details in their schedules. On the other hand they also typically use sub-contractors, and often own specific procurement aspects.

Although many of the concepts described herein are independent of whether SAP is part of the mix or not, my assumption here is that this is the case.

In principle the solution is defined by a master schedule managed by the GC in Primavera, derived from the sales-driven high-level budgetary structure coming out of SAP. Sub-contractors may manage lower level schedules.

I have seen GCs manage two levels of schedule in the Primavera environment. One is a master schedule, linked to detailed schedules. The master schedule is the one reported to the owner. It contains general milestones, summary progress information, and billing-related information. The master schedule is to be derived from SAP and expanded on during project execution. It is also to be integrated into the owner's schedule - with a requirement for a potential secondary integration solution (see above, owner-managed capital projects).

Although there are many similarities to the owner-managed capital projects solution, the different focus on details of the schedule will have an impact on business scenarios and detailed mappings.

Key Functional Characteristics.

- SAP contains high-level structure and budget and revenue information (i.e. as a master schedule)
- Selection of scope by project
- Division of overall project into sub-projects
- Relationship between financially controlled cost breakdown structure (CBS - becomes high level WBS in Master Schedule) and schedule-driven work breakdown structure (WBS - as details of Master Schedule and in detailed Project Schedules)
- Integration into sales, with either time-based or progress-based or milestone-based billings
- Strong use of sub-contractors to deliver sub-projects
- Project Progress and Earned-Value Type reporting requirements
- Internally provided resources to be loaded into Primavera
- Procurement relationship to sub-contractors to be considered
- Physical integration of contractor schedules, or sharing of schedules in one environment
- Contractors may not always use the same scheduling tool (e.g. MS Project or Primavera)
- Primavera contains general contractor's schedules

- Frequency of updates is smaller than with outages, typically once a week
- Data volume may be big, but performance requirements are more relaxed than comparable turnarounds, due to the lower frequency
- Sign-off processes on progress, including related reconciliation with procurement
- Integration of Primavera schedule with SAP procurement activities for labor and materials

Options. The following functionality is optional and depends on the specific business processes to be reflected:

- Sharing of Primavera Master Schedules with owners to enable bottom-up push of project progress information
- Primavera (Master Schedule) to Primavera (Detailed Schedule) integration
- Variations of progress updates are possible (e.g. units, physical inspection, duration-based)

Recommended or Required Add-ons and Enhancements. For the general contractor-managed service projects schedule, the highest-value challenges to be tackled by add-ons deal with the management of the procurement aspects of multi-level schedules, to be clear about progress, reconciliation of with sub-project schedules, and to determine risks for schedule and cost overruns.

- Conditional Updates
- API Enhancements (i.e. integration into procurement processes)
- Advanced Solution Templates (i.e. split into multi-level schedules)
- Resources Transfer

Depending on the depth of the integration, the data volume of integration may warrant considering additional transfer management capabilities:

- Transfer Controls
- Transfer Performance Optimization
- Transfer Preview and Simulation

Future Functionality. The above describes common and proven solution components for general contractor-managed service projects. Technology and advanced principles enable the following additional functions and features, which further could enhance the overall value of such a solution.

- List of scheduled activities and feedback should be fed directly to individual end users (i.e. through mobile technology)
- Automated consolidation of contractor schedules into the owner's master schedule

Make-to-Order Projects

Business Context. Make-to-Order projects manage the production and delivery of a product for a customer. Examples could be the creation of a new power generator, or a port or dam. Although there are various options of commercial and organizational arrangements, the underlying assumption is that both the Primavera and the SAP system are owned by the same organization, and that this organization has the overall responsibility to deliver the project result. In most cases this would be a discrete manufacturing company, working primarily with internal personnel and subcontractors.

In a systems-of-systems context some of the components of the overall solution may be produced externally. Their schedule would then need to be integrated into the overall schedule. A prime example of this is ***the*** "complex project", the development of complex aircraft like the Joint Strike Fighter (JSF) F-35.

This multi-billion-dollar project was in reality a program in which up to multi-billion-dollar components were contracted out. At the beginning of the project some of the technologies to be used were not even invented or developed themselves. The project was in reality a program with an overall Program Schedule, consisting of Component Schedules that can also be called Master Schedules. Those Master Projects were broken out into ever-lower levels, with decentralized responsibilities but integrated schedules.

Make-to-Order projects do not always need to be that big, of course, and may even be managed totally in-house. It is also perceivable that complete make-to-order solutions for the purpose of the implementation of a SAP-Primavera integration solution are in reality the equivalent of component schedules for a much larger project at the customer side. In the above example, the development of an aircraft engine for the U.S. Department of Defense may be considered a component project for the overall JSF development effort.

Key Functional Characteristics.

- Multi-level Schedules in SAP and in Primavera (multiple ones in Primavera)
- Link to SAP Sales & Distribution (SD) sales orders
- Specific reporting requirements for the client
- Detailed status controls across applications
- Creation of activities and resource assignments
- Top down communication of high-level schedule dates and milestones
- Summarization of resource assignments
- Bottom-up calculation to derive progress for higher levels

Options.

- Link to sub-contractors' detailed schedules (component schedules in a systems-of-systems context)
- Advanced cost-based integration to facilitate official earned value standards
- Multiple levels of details for resource assignments and resource-loaded scheduling

Add-ons and Enhancements.

- Conditional Updates
- API Enhancements, i.e. for sales and procurement integration, and download of resources
- Transfer Management to consider high data volume
- Primavera (Master Schedule) to Primavera (Master Schedule) integration
- Custom Transactions

- Custom Error Handling
- Performance Optimization
- Transfer Simulation

Future.

- List of scheduled activities and feedback should be fed directly to individual end users (i.e. through mobile technology)
- Automated consolidation of contractor schedules into the owner's master schedule

Routine Maintenance

Business Context. The main integration challenge of Routine Maintenance events is to determine a high-level project schedule about six weeks in advance and a detailed short-term look-ahead work schedule covering about two weeks in advance. To get to that point, and still leave some flexibility to react to last-minute changes in requirements, the grouping of work is either done by a project or a revision.

The assignment and re-assignment of work needs to be done in either application. However, it is more likely to be done in Primavera, among other reasons since a by-and-large fixed group of resources is being used to perform routine maintenance work.

The scope of work is built using a list of long-term work activities, associated with equipment and functional locations. Based on related task lists and triggered by notifications, the respective work orders are built. Managed primarily by detailed status controls in SAP and Primavera, the six-week schedule is built by pushing data into Primavera.

The rest of the project is mainly handled in Primavera, where schedulers use a large number of activity codes and user-defined fields to sort and group and slice and dice the overall body of work and assign the best priorities for the short-term work schedule. This data is presented to the maintenance work teams who report back hours (through SAP) and progress (in Primavera).

The Routine Maintenance processes may include the assignment of individuals in Primavera.

This work is similar to operational work. Rarely parts of the work are critical to be performed at a very specific date, although the maintenance window for any specific piece of equipment is overall relatively well defined.

Key Functional Characteristics.

- Selection of scope by revision or project
- Separation between planning (in SAP) and scheduling (in Primavera)
- Typically two levels of schedules in Primavera (6 weeks out and skill-based resource assignment, and 2 weeks out with more detailed or even individual resource assignments)
- Resources coming from SAP
- Resource assignments done either in SAP or in Primavera
- Initial relationships coming from SAP during activity creation, then Primavera takes over
- Status control from SAP (ready to schedule)
- Re-assignments in Primavera are possible
- Limited consideration of materials
- Resources may include rented equipment like cranes
- No earned value calculations necessary since this is more similar to operational work than to projects

Options.

- Updating of the number of resources used may either be done in SAP or in Primavera
- The geospatial location of work may be integrated into the work orders, using custom fields
- There is at least one ABAP-based tool available that can address short-term scheduling requirement in the SAP-PM application, the Graphical Scheduler offered by Prometheus Group. The specific value assessment of Primavera, or its scope to cover part of the overall process, should be assessed by the client.

Add-ons and Enhancements.

- Conditional Updates
- Transfer Preview and Simulations
- API Enhancements
- Missing Order Identification
- Resources Transfer

Future.

Technology and advanced principles enable the following additional functions and features, which further could enhance the overall value of the solution.

- List of scheduled activities and feedback should be fed directly to individual end users (i.e. through mobile technology)
- Real-time feedback loops from individual users to feed back progress to schedulers, planners, and management (i.e. through mobile technology)

6.

DOING. DOING. DONE! IMPLEMENT SMARTLY

Definition of Success: Smiling Faces

When I walk into a project from the outside, I usually rather quickly pick out several key client team members as my core customers. Then I try to picture them with genuinely smiling faces. And then I try to make this reality. There may be different reasons why they smile, but smile they should nevertheless.

The Business is Smiling.

Take you as the representative of the business. I want you to smile because you are convinced that you really got the solution you needed, and because you are surprised about how well it went and how solid and capable it feels. Your original vision may have started out more like a dream using a number of qualifiers ("ideally", "at some point", "it would be great"). The result likely is not the same as you pictured yourself, for reasons I am explaining in more detail above, in Step 5 and below in Myth No. 4.

It was more detailed work than anticipated, but because of that you are now confident of what you achieved. What you got feels a bit like that dream come true. Something that works. Something that makes the Primavera users happy without alienating the SAP users. Something that drives SAP data to Primavera without burdening the schedulers.

Both sides of the application world are happy. Finance is happy. So you are happy also.

IT is Smiling.

And there is you from IT, realizing that you were capable to make something really tricky work. You managed even though you never had heard of this ominous SAP EPC application before, and although Primavera really is not your strong suit. What happened is that the installation of some application turned out to be no less than 15 pieces and subcomponents having to work with each other like cogs in a wheel.

At times it was difficult to come up with the best decisions since the implications were so unclear. However, it worked and now you have a well-performing robust, powerful and scalable solution that makes your end-users feel good. The solution is a true business enabler and generates an ROI that a pure interface could not deliver even remotely.

No budget overrun, but just a well-functioning IT-enabled solution. Some of the good stuff.

The Project Manager is Smiling.

Even you, the project manager, are happy. What first looked like a simple "interface project" revealed an awfully large number of complex pieces and required demanding coordination of many different parties and experts. When you look back, though, you realize that the profoundly complicated stuff was never the real issue.

It was effectively taken care of for two main reasons:

(1) You used the right team of experienced people working with a proven methodology and a set of mature tools.

(2) By following the six steps in this book, particularly the implementation checklists, the task had become smooth, with next to no surprises.

Yes, no-surprises usually make it fun for a project manager.

Project Management Methodology

The implementation approach and methodology matter big time. With Project Management lots of the success factors are brought together. If you define the project from Step 1 through Step 6, as outlined here, it will be hard work but things will fall in place and you will generate superb business value.

Keep the strategic goals in mind - integrating SAP and Primavera is about more effectively using projects to execute strategic business objectives. This can make the difference between surviving as a business and not, between staying competitive, adjusting and adapting, or becoming obsolete. With that as the backdrop, shortcuts should not be part of your repertoire.

All the steps need to be methodically performed, with attention to detail and considering a wide array of technical, functional, process and business aspects. You do that with good project management yourself.

Like in any good project, you should follow multiple phases with clear activities and distinct deliverables. I will list them on the following pages. You should by now discover the various activities and understand how they relate to the whole picture.

Project Management Approach

The typical implementation of a complete SAP-Primavera integration solution takes about 4 to 8 months. In very complex organizations this can easily double, e.g. when business processes need to be standardized or configuration in SAP is changed during the implementation of the SAP-Primavera integration solution.

A Contractor-Run World.

My recommendation is to keep project management in-house, seriously empower the project manager, and establish effective controls over all contractors. It usually pays off to run the project in a team approach and to not put an artificial middle layer in the mix, like a systems integrator (SI), purely to manage a team of outside experts and coordinate activities. Watch out, there is a potential trap here!

Implementing SAP-Primavera integration at a major oil company in Calgary, Canada, I was concerned when I noticed that the project timeline kept slipping and the budget kept creeping up. However, this did not seem to be an issue. Surprise?

The mystery was resolved when the project team agreed on another extension of the timeline and budget, and we asked who would need to approve that.

It became apparent that every project team member was a supplier or contractor, and even the majority of the users were contracted. Simply put, it was in everybody's self interest to take pressure off, increase scope and ask for more budget. And since nobody outside the project team had independent insight in the project, and all project team members were contractors, they (we) essentially voted for more money to themselves (ourselves).

This does not mean that the decisions were wrong. There were controls in place that aligned the project manager's role to corporate interests, in a way that an employee could hardly have done better. Further, it really did make sense to focus on delivering a better product when opportunities were identified or unexpected issues came up. The cost-benefit was obvious, and the project manager acted ethically and clearly kept the customer's interest as the prime responsibility at all times. Also, the budget owner could of course theoretically still have stopped the project.

For all these reasons I consider the above to have worked out just right for the customer and the delivered value was the higher for it. This is not always the case, though. Frequently I encounter situations where suppliers and contractors provide almost all IT functions. Lots of time can be wasted by wading through service level agreements (SLAs) and established practices and processes that were not designed with support for a SAP-Primavera integration project at mind.

Just ask yourself: Who provides the hardware? Who installs the operating system and database? Who installs Primavera? Who maintains the SAP ECC system? Who maintains the network? Who is providing post-Go Live support? Beyond that, who is providing the functional SAP support, for one module or the other? And who does the same for Primavera?

The answer to all these questions could be: "Our IT Department", or it could be: "8 or 9 different suppliers and contractors". If the situation is closer to the second one, then this hardly can efficiently be resolved by throwing the responsibility to coordinate at yet another supplier, like an SI. Such an entity is likely interpreted as a potential competitor and lacks the ability to cut through the fog with authority.

Not doing so is likely to lead to more delays and frustrations, more effort spent on coordination, inefficient use of resources, larger risk margins, and thus to higher costs and longer time frames.

Onsite vs. Offsite

Many clients have been conditioned over decades that implementations of enterprise business applications require:

(A) Work to be done onsite, and

(B) Work to be measured in "man-months" or "man-weeks".

The truth is that it can be a huge advantage when an experienced team with proven tools can hit the ground running offsite. One gets the best of many worlds, access to a large number of resources, rapid development due to the use of an established infrastructure, and optimized processes for the most critical early phases of a project.

Offsite work, particularly when paired with an offsite infrastructure, eliminates dependencies on a client's IT department, or procurement processes, or corporate standards in peripheral manners. POCs and prototypes can be performed much more effectively, and it is easier to validate design decisions.

Not all work should be done offsite, though. There always is a role for client interaction, particularly during workshops early on. This is when ideally the full team is present. It is very important to get everybody on the same page and develop a personal relationship. After a couple of personal meetings, this is no longer as important anymore.

Then collaboration and communication technologies kick in, and overall productivity can be enhanced when people do not have to block out big chunks of time for meetings. Even more, test cycles can be sped up significantly. I have several times been involved in projects where the technical team was located in a different time zone. The result was that during the day testing was performed by business users, in the evening (morning for the techies) the issues were discussed, and by the next morning "the fix was in".

Can it get any better?

Project Phases

Toward a Realistic Project Plan

Considering the strategic nature and value of an integrated schedule, and its potentially huge impact on the corporate bottom-line or your organization's ability to effectively execute on corporate strategies, put together a realistic implementation plan. Assume that logistically little of substance and organizational and technical complexity can be done in an enterprise organization within a timeframe faster than three months, and that usually it takes about twice as long.

Assume a multi-phase project and roughly one to two months for scoping and design, one to two months for building the solution, one to two months for properly testing it, and another one to two months to train, cutover, and go live. Roughly you will end up with an overall duration of between 4 and 8 months. At times it can be done faster, at times it will be slower. It should never be much faster, and never be much slower.

The reason is that even in vastly varying detailed circumstances the overall complexity of the job does not differ too much. When using the right tools and team, it is the thinking and discussing, mocking up, trying out, building, reviewing and testing that takes most of the time, and rarely how complicated a specific decision or solution component is.

Considering that, try not to implement much faster for the sake of it. You may be missing something critical or reduce quality. It is better to let the business and IT digest options and solution components properly. Do also not try to go much slower since it rarely is necessary except in special circumstances. The six-step process described in this book is very similar across most solutions. A benefit of its complexity is then that the overall effort can be more predicted realistically within a reasonable margin.

Prepare, assume 5 phases that use on average between 2 and 3 outside experts for a duration of between 4 and 8 months, and execute.

Preparation: Tactical Alignment

Before you jump into the actual implementation of the solution, take a breather and perform the equivalent of a feasibility study, conceptual design, or pre-design effort: Figure out the general outline of what you want to do. Then tackle the technical, commercials and procurement tasks required to be ready with internal resources, hardware, software and external services.

Duration. Take about a month of time for this, followed by cleaning up all logistical requirements.

Project Activities. During the tactical alignment phase, make sure you properly address the below 15 parameters. Then take the outcome, put it together in form of a project charter and as the basis for a request for proposal or statement of work. Sort out the paperwork and logistical aspects, and be ready to kick off the project.

1. Integration Platform.
2. Buy versus Build.
3. Supportability.
4. Software Versions and Releases.
5. Technical Landscape.
6. Data Volume and Performance Expectation.
7. Generic Process Flow.
8. Object-Level Mappings.
9. Number of Schedules.
10. Reporting Requirements.
11. Data Conversion.
12. Implementation Cost Estimate.
13. Implementation Time Estimate.
14. Organizational Context.
15. Engagement Approach.

Deliverables.

- Project Charter
- Procurement Documents
- Project Team

Phase 1: Scope Verification

Use a Scope Verification Phase, to review the high-level scope and project parameters, covering process, functionality and technical aspects. It can be tempting to cut short scope verification, or even cut it out. Don't do that, since it not just helps kicking off the project properly, but it also results in valuable deliverables that set the stage for the detailed design.

Duration. The tentative duration of the scope verification phase is two to four weeks. This considers a review of written materials, analysis of data, onsite workshops. It also includes the review of high-level specifications like the validation of APIs and of the SAP and Primavera design impacting the solution.

Project Activities.

- Project Kickoff
- Project Plan Review, covering technical and functional activities in SAP ECC, EPC and Primavera
- On-site Scope Validation Workshop of between 3 and 5 days
- Off-site documentation, calls, and short clarification workshops
- Validation of general technical and functional requirements, i.e.
  - Selection criteria and project definition
  - Basic workflow
  - Object-level mappings
  - Technical landscape implication
  - Approach to performance optimization
  - Error handling
- Analysis of sample data sets
- Preparation of demos (system setup)
- Validation of technical solution landscape
- System access for all team members, including remote access
- Review of SAP and Primavera systems, including configuration

Deliverables. Typical deliverables produced during the Scope Verification Phase are:

- Documentation of generic process flow and object-level mappings
- Documentation of generic mappings
- Documentation of key requirements having been analyzed and validated
- Agreement on key items of the project plan, and understanding of dependencies
- Documentation standards

- Detailed definition of the technical landscape, including software versions and releases

Phase 2: Detailed Design

The Detailed Design Phase is arguably the most critical phase of an implementation. This is where the specifications funnel is in full action. Take the high-level and general object-level and process design, and derive very detailed specifications of mappings and logical conditions.

This includes multiple walks through the complete project life cycle, providing up to six different perspectives as outlined above. It is also the time to review sample data and the configuration and setup of SAP and Primavera.

This is a chance to dive into details, get input from various business units, and review in great detail whether the design is acceptable to the business. Keep the long-term goal in mind, which implies that you do not just want to design for one pilot even if only one site will go live initially. The implementation of a SAP-Primavera integration solution can drive process standardization, and this is the phase where such decisions can and should be made.

Duration. The tentative duration of the detailed design phase is four to six weeks. If the complexity of an enterprise organization is higher, and to get input and sign-off from various business units or locations, it is wise to extend this time period.

Project Activities. The main challenge during the detailed design is to ensure that full and formal agreement on all specifications has been reached. You achieve that through:

- On-site workshop(s) to clarify detailed design specifications (ca. 4 to 8 days, covering one or two weeks)
- Documentation of detailed design specifications (MS Excel Mapping Spreadsheet)
- Development of an advanced prototype to reflect the requirements as understood

- Walk through the prototype to validate requirements and finalize the detailed design
- Definition of unit test scenarios and scripts
- Installation of software components, including add-ons, enhancements and accelerators, in the client development environment (may miss pieces that need to be finalized, e.g. relating to performance optimization)

Deliverables. Typical deliverables produced during the Detailed Design Phase are:

- Functional Design Specifications document in form of a detailed mapping spreadsheet
- Demonstration and joint review of high-level prototype, built in the implementer's environment
- Validation and documentation of specs
- Definition of unit test scripts

Phase 3: Build

The Build Phase involves the coding, assembling and configuring of the solution according to the detailed design specifications. I have seen this most successfully done as a two-step process.

First it is all about taking the prototype, which hopefully was performed during the detailed design, and integrate all additional requirements as completely as possible. This should be done in an open environment, not having to consider any dependencies on other technical teams, procurement, or procedures and policies.

Essentially it requires the use of a remote development environment provided by the implementers. The result of this first step is that the overwhelming majority of the functionality has been built as rapidly and as flexibly as possible, unit tested according to the pre-defined unit test scenarios. Ideally there would not be any setup and configuration differences to the client development environment, but there always are some, and those need to be tackled next.

In the second step the solution is then implemented in the client development environment. At that point, the technical team should have had more than two months since project kickoff. It should have been able to set up, in conjunction with an installation consultant, a well-functioning development environment.

As the advanced and almost complete solution from step one gets installed, it will deal with the technical, configuration and data idiosyncrasies of the client's environment. This is a very critical task, and it will require a formal review of unit test scenarios. The best approach there is to have the developers and implementers walk through the unit test scripts first, and fix issues. The formal sign-off on the built solution is best done by the business performing the unit test scripts themselves, with the implementers looking over their shoulders.

It is essential to hit the second step as soon as possible, as what I call "idiosyncrasies" always exists and may throw some wrinkles in an otherwise well-built solution. Those should be confronted sooner rather than later. However, and this is very important to keep in mind: If step one is rushed, this can lead to the opposite effect that is desired.

It is likely to prolong and complicate the implementation process. The reason is the invariable slowdown triggered through the introduction of complexities and dependencies on other systems, people and activities. Components of the technical environment need to be shared, and technical and business teams are still on a steep learning curve.

Duration. The tentative duration of the build phase is four to six weeks.

Project Activities. The main challenge during the detailed design is to build and deliver all formally defined specifications. This requires:

- Completion of EPC setup and tailoring efforts, reflecting all requirements from the detailed design
- Documentation of the installation effort
- Functional unit testing and walk through unit test scenarios (developers/implementers, and business team)

- Drafts of detailed documentation of ABAP, XSLT and Java Components, and related know-how transfer
- Setup of the test or quality assurance environment

Deliverables. Typical deliverables produced during the Build Phase are:

- Unit tests to document formal delivery according to specs
- Draft documentation of ABAP, XSLT, and Java work, and begin of related know-how transfer sessions
- Installation of remaining software components, e.g. for performance optimization

Note:

It is understandable that during the Build phase there is a desire of the client's team (technical and business) to frequently interact with the developers, get frequent detailed updates, and to push them toward getting their job done as soon as possible. Please be patient. It usually does not help. I have seen clients push and distract, interfering with best practices, resulting in an overall slowdown of the implementation time.

For example, deploying a half-finished solution too early in the client's system will slow down the implementation process in almost all cases.

Phase 4: Validation

"Validation" is a nice word for gradually hitting the solution ever harder and weirder and more unorthodox to really make sure it can stand the onslaught of the real world out there. That real world consists of large numbers of data, sometimes surprising and unusual data, untypical business situations, an unexpected sequence of tasks, and a range of technical issues and interdependencies that are not easy to anticipate. To reflect this, the solution will be unit tested in a controlled environment, then unit tested in a shared environment, then informally integration tested, then formally integration tested, then user acceptance tested, and performance tested, and authorization tested, and regression tested. Then you are ready for prime time.

During the Validation Phase you as the client need to take over ever more responsibility. If local business consultants are involved, this is their opportunity to shine also. The outside development experts should be fixing things only, not drive anything anymore.

The Validation phase also provides an excellent ground to train up support personnel. Use it that way. The reason is simple: Testing is about figuring out what works and does not work, identifying the exact issues, and communicating them to the technical development team. This is very similar to the Level 1 - Level 2 - External Support arrangement that in one form or another may occur during the post-Go Live.

The more works the easier it gets. Until then it is about testing, analyzing, supporting, fixing, and re-testing.

Duration. The tentative duration of the validation phase is six to ten weeks. If necessary to consider the complexity of an enterprise organization, and to get input and sign-off from various business units or locations, it can be wise to extend this time period.

Project Activities. The main challenge during the validation phase is to ensure that the solution has been tested and found satisfactory to be used by end users and real types and quantities of data. The satisfaction of functionality is mostly measured in SAP and Primavera, with EPC just being the conduit enabling it to happen. Activities involve at a minimum:

- Two or three integration test and related fix cycles, with a duration of one to two weeks each
- Two or three user acceptance test and related fix cycles, with a duration of one to two weeks each
- Additional know-how transfer sessions to enable support of the solution, as required
- Final delivery of documentation about ABAP, XSLT and Java Components

Deliverables. Typical deliverables produced during the Validation Phase are:

- Executed and documented test scripts
- List of issues and their resolution

Phase 5: Cutover and Go Live

During the Cutover and Go-Live Phase the technical support and the business team should in theory be self-sufficient. The project team's main role is to be available in case of any unusual issues during the technical cut-over itself, and to be able to quickly address support issues when new users work with the new solution for the first time. Ideally it is mainly about making a good first impression, no matter what.

Duration. The tentative duration of Cutover and Go Live typically is between two and six weeks. This is somewhat flexible, and depends on how much formal early-Go Live support you want to provide to the users.

Project Activities. The main challenge during Cutover is to validate ensure that the technical team has performed the correct steps at this critical juncture. Other than that, post-Go Live is about having capable team members on standby in case of issues.

Deliverables. General support services, typically on standby and ad-hoc.

Post-Go Live: Support

"Most issues with business software applications are interface issues." I heard this once at Marathon Oil in Findlay, Ohio. Jeff Heath described most such issues as "interface issues, meaning they are caused by the interface between the chair and the keyboard". Based on my personal experience in what I personally define as "technical issues", that about sums it up.

Our challenge for providing post-Go Live support is to know the difference between the above interface issues, which is the human element, and real technical issues relating to EPC, and everything in-between. Then we are to provide an approach for helping to resolve each one of them.

Every implementation of an integrated SAP-Primavera solution should aim at making the client as independent as possible from specialized outside support. That is not just a noble goal, it is a necessary one. You as the customer need to own the solution.

However, support of a complex solution like this one has many levels. All of those need to be considered. Let's first look at the potential technical issues, all of which an IT department should be able to support directly, through standard arrangements with vendors, or using an internal Center of Excellence:

1. Hardware issues
2. Network issues
3. Operating system issues
4. Database issues
5. SAP ECC functional issues
6. SAP ECC Basis System/technical issues
7. SAP ECC authorization issues
8. Primavera P6 functional issues
9. Primavera P6 technical issues
10. Primavera P6 API, or API Server, technical issues
11. SAP API issues
12. SAP EPC platform issues

From that point on it gets a bit harder, since now the specific business logic needs to be considered. If you have an issue, is it really due the XSLT in EPC, and if yes, what exactly is the issue? How do you find out? How does the user find out?

The first step to address this is by including in the solution design the ability to manually correct as many issues as possible that realistically can be expected to come up. The second step is to provide good error handling capabilities. What is left should be rare. It probably is also more complicated to analyze, and requires a look at more detailed and more technical logs.

It could be that the logic works according to specifications and exactly as designed, but that the data set is incorrect. It could also be user error in the sense that somebody did not follow the training script, or violated operating procedures. It could also be a data set that is different than expected. "It could" be so many things, even once the above dozen technical reasons are excluded, that the support process needs to focus on the "could" much more than on the ability for fixing complicated technical details that only very rarely will be required.

What you realistically can expect is thorough documentation, effective know-how transfer for how to analyze and interpret the vast majority of issues, and proper tools to address them.

What realistically cannot be expected in most cases is that this will allow your support organization to make significant changes to the solution without external support and a lot of additional practice and learning. Theoretically it would be possible, but one would need to maintain a specialized team who understand an interface that hardly ever changes.

In most solution implementations I have seen, the costs of bringing and keeping all that know-how on site is almost never justifiable. One can get a long way, though, and almost all organizations I have worked with are substantially independent of external support.

Keep in mind that the integration really is a "solution" to a complex process challenge. You had to align processes in SAP and Oracle-Primavera, match terminology and concepts, and standardize business rules. All of that was based on the assumption of a specific configuration of either one of these applications, and of a specific nature of data sets that by-and-large remain stable over a large period of time.

Changes to such a solution should not be under-estimated, and should not be part of the expectation for support.

List of Key Conditions

The above implementation timelines depend on conditions, some of the most important ones are:

- Prompt system access for all team members
- Remote system access for the technical and functional consultants
- ABAP developer keys for the technical consultants
- Full administrative server access to the NetWeaver/EPC server

- Full user access for the technical and functional consultants in SAP and Primavera (admin or admin-like access in the development environment)
- Representative test data available in development (some) and test environments (a lot)
- Complete and technically validated development systems landscape available two weeks before the end of the Detailed Design Phase
- Complete and technical validated test systems landscape available two weeks before the end of the Build Phase
- Knowledge transfer is done as a continuing process, using a combination of documentation and short-term interactive sessions, and not as formal training
- Most implementation or implementation support work is likely to be done remotely, to prevent too many people hanging around for what often is part-time contributions only
- Until the Build Phase is complete, the main development environment to be used is likely to be hosted by the implementers
- Prompt decision making by the client's business and technical teams

Helpful Real-life Lessons Learned

In this book I talk about a very large number of considerations and steps to prevent major mishaps or misjudgments as you start your effort to implement an SAP-Primavera integration solution. The following lists a few specific learnings that have proven to be key for success. There is no particular sequence, and each implementation may be different, though.

1. Use external environments for demos during the design process, to allow for quality design input including "see, touch and feel" of real systems.
2. Use external environments to enable rapid development without a solid dependency on a local technical

landscape to be established, or on the learning curve of people new to the overall solution.

3. Use a prototyping approach to feed back key process, functional and technical elements to the business before commencing the final development push in a Build Phase.

4. Do not introduce authorization control too early, particularly not into a development environment, to not slow down the core development effort.

5. Consider resource availability and related costs for a staged cutover and roll-out approach.

6. Address all contract negotiations and logistics for all involved vendors promptly, and get them concluded before the formal start of the project.

7. Think through test scripts early in the process to ensure that a formalized scope definition covering realistic business scenarios and related actions in SAP and Primavera are made an intricate part of the development cycle.

8. Include sufficient P6 expertise for the project, and ideally keep it inside the organization, not just some scheduler with one set of experiences.

9. Put significant focus on the quality of the design documentation, by focusing on low-level details following walk-throughs of the project life-cycle, SAP and Primavera configuration, and specific data sets at the client.

10. Stay aware that users of an SAP-Primavera integration solution primarily perform actions in the SAP and Primavera applications, resulting in a need to standardize processes and drive an organizational change management strategy.

11. Make sure the roles and responsibilities of a systems integrator are clearly defined and accepted by the client and the implementer's personnel, in advance of the implementation.

12. Address early on typical afterthoughts, i.e. reporting requirements in SAP and Primavera, user-friendliness and support requirements, and performance expectations.

Bonus Features.
MYTHBUSTERS: THE 8 DEADLY SINS

Myth 1. "It's an installation, not an implementation"

Here we go. This is one of the biggest and most frequent misperception when it comes to SAP-Primavera integration. It is when a technical team is tasked with "implementing" a software product, essentially installing it, instead of making the delivery of tangible business value front, center and back of the solution.

Let's look at the following example, which I have frequently encountered in several variations.

The Business Leads.

An enterprise organization has a pain point of disjointed schedules, incomplete reporting and inefficient resource usage. This has resulted in frequent cost and schedule overruns, or quality issues, or both, without visibility into the specific root causes. There is no consistent ability to manage and prevent such issues from occurring the first place.

It has been determined that the issue is an inability to provide correct information at the right time to the right people.

So far so good.

Then the business starts digging for solutions. Somebody vaguely remembers Impress, talks to Oracle and hears about Inspire, may even hear from SAP that they have a product called EPC. Reading up on those, one cannot be otherwise than be bolstered by aggressive, and while not strictly speaking incorrect still often misleading, marketing literature. All said solutions are supposed to be proven, easy to deploy, and having tons of out-of-the-box capabilities including hundreds of default mappings.

Enter IT.

Satisfied that there seem capable solutions on the market, at that point the business hands the job on to IT with the marching order to evaluate further, and then "find and give us an interface". And here we go (I am repeating myself).

IT does what it does best. They look at the solution as an interface and get ready to "put it in". IT may even discover that they own the licenses to EPC already. Instead of looking for solution experts and an experienced implementation partner, they try out installing it themselves.

With the help of the software vendor they succeed with the installation, see dozens or even hundreds of fields coming across, thinking "that was easy". They got pretty far, at least so it seems.

In the extreme case it even is enough to declare victory and move on. Mission accomplished, the interface is there, people should be able to use it, so get on with it!

Next project, please.

The Cycle Continues.

If it just were so easy.

The above rarely gets one anywhere. After all, we are not talking about downloading an iPad app and installing it and off we go making airline reservations, checking the weather in far away places, or reading a newspaper. This directly affects work, directly affects business and the bottom line.

Where are the users? Where is the business? Where is the bottom line?

An implementation requires real commitment of the business, analyses, thinking, process standardization, evaluations of business scenarios and a walk through detailed data, processes and reports.

By treating this as a technical exercise no tangible value is generated. Another costly endeavor ends up on the landfill of "technical failures". I see that often at clients that have tried a large number of "interfaces". Some succeed reasonably well, but many have "tried them all and none work". It usually is SAP's fault, or Impress' or the consultant's.

What I see is that it rarely is that simple.

> **LEARNING.** Treating the building of an integrated schedule as an installation rather than an implementation hardly ever works.
>
> Handing it off to IT hardly ever delivers the real value, particularly when it is combined with an unrealistic budget and time expectation (see Myth 3).
>
> The business team needs to consist of a visible and involved customer. It also needs to have a serious commitment in people, money and time, and lead the implementation effort throughout the whole process.
>
> (This goes for any tool you would pick, not just SAP EPC.)

Myth 2. "The out-of-the-box is almost good enough"

Let me give the short answer first. Although I like the notion of, and believe in, the positive context of "Yes we can", the answer is "no".

The misperception is about what the out-of-the-box is. It is a platform with a bunch of sample code in a one-size-fits-all and none-of-your-specific-processes-matters package.

This myth sometimes is, knowingly or unknowingly, perpetuated by software vendors. In the case of SAP EPC, the marketing and sales pitch is that it comes with this wonderful platform (agreed!) and hundreds of out-of-the-box mappings (yes!) that are put together in a template that is based on a real-life implementation (correct!).

If all of these statements are right, why would I call it a myth?

It is because of the insinuation that the above would be meaningful enough to deliver an integrated schedule in a quick, simple, cheap and almost effortless exercise. In almost all cases nothing can be further from the truth.

Keep in mind what SAP does when offering one template for "PS integration" and one template for "PM integration", using only standard BAPIs.

They don't differentiate, for example:

- Between processes, like make-to-order versus capital versus engineering and construction versus service delivery, or routine maintenance versus a refueling outage versus a turnaround.
- Between industries, like oil & gas versus utilities versus railroads versus chemicals versus aerospace and defense.
- Between configuration and process definition in SAP and Primavera, like planning in SAP versus Primavera, heavy use of activity codes in Primavera versus using Primavera as a reporting tool, resource management in Primavera or SAP, etc.
- Between different levels of functional requirements: resource integration, multiple levels of schedules in Primavera, one-to-many mappings, rolling up of object mappings, etc.

Do you really think one size fits all, or even nearly all?

When you read my self-congratulatory list of experience in various industries, processes, etc. - do you really think all of those could have been handled with a bit of tweaking of one basic set of sample code?

Going beyond that, a single out-of-the-box template cannot deal with performance, advanced error handling, transfer controls, reports, multi-threading, batching, connecting multiple environments, adding additional object links, missing orders, advanced logic transformation like WBS, changing the sequence of processes, introducing conditional updates, or any kind of customization.

Out-of-the-box does not differentiate between the handling of linear assets vs. a regular outage, or between an owner-based control of schedules vs. a general contractor controlled one.

What about status controls along the project life cycle? Or the handling of multiple levels of schedules? The various ways of reporting progress? It does not consider integration into other modules like SAP Human Resources or Procurement, or Controlling.

Add to that the fact that there is hardly any link between complexity and number of mappings, and believing incorrectly interpreting the marketing and sales talk can lead to huge misunderstandings in the best case, and gross failures in the worst.

What one needs to do is gather requirements first, and then go to the drawing board, follow a formal and comprehensive design process, use capable add-ons and enhancements, and then deliver realistically and powerfully.

The out-of-the-box template is not much more than an example. Basing an implementation, or even a proof-of-concept, on the EPC out-of-the-box template is an unrealistic exercise that does not give EPC the due respect for the power and scalability of its platform, while quite likely drawing unrealistic and possibly negative conclusions while doing so.

LEARNING. For a real enterprise-level and industrial-strength solution, the out-of-the-box EPC template never is even close to be sufficient. Usually it requires a profound re-design using new workflows and a different sequence of steps and object-level mappings, plus substantial modifications and enhancements to reflect specific business requirements and to turn a rudimentary solution into one that really is "robust", "industrial-strength" or "enterprise-ready".

The out-of-the-box EPC template is not even sufficient for a POC, and when used that way is likely to lead to incorrect conclusions that underestimate the platform's capabilities and grossly misjudge the actual implementation effort.

Myth 3. "Too much money – we can do it cheaper"

A True Story.

It happened several times like that.

I estimate the effort and cost it takes to integrate schedules for the management of turnarounds in a multi-billion dollar corporation with over one dozen plants, quoting several hundred thousand dollars to achieve the goal to save between one million and three million dollars per turnaround event - and all I hear is deafening silence.

Then the predictable next steps: Challenging the premises of the quotes (Myth No. 1, Myth No. 2, and Myth No. 4), taking more time to decide (Myth No. 6), asking for an "EPC consultant" to pick up some skills on the cheap (Myth No. 5), and the ultimate fallback of tasking IT to do it themselves (Myth No. 8). While doing so, arguments question line items of a few days of effort here, or of the value of powerful add-ons, enhancements and pre-build solution components there.

Let me get this straight: You want to integrate enterprise business applications from SAP and Oracle and you think this can be done on the cheap? Why, because SAP is easy? Or because your business is easy?

Being able to do "it" cheaper most often is a myth. You either pay now, or pay later and more. Cut out time during design or during testing challenges the quality of the solution and may even seriously risk the project. Users may not be properly considered, pre-existing solution components may need to be invented again at significant cost. Timelines get extended, the maturity of the solution is reduced, functions and features may be missing, even the basic layout of the solution may be in question.

Is that really worth it?

Or is it being Penny-wise and Pound-foolish?

Penny-wise and...

What gets me is that many of these organizations frequently seem less stressed out about spending the money otherwise. Real-life examples I have seen is spending far over $10,000 to establish a remote access Citrix connection (a one hour effort?), or accepting four week lead times to spend a few hours supporting the installation of a server, interrupting and restarting a project for several months to buy and install a hard drive, or to hire 10 to 20 SAP consultants for a period of several years of full-time engagement to improve on an already existing asset management solution.

This statement often is coupled with "we only need [xyz] mappings" and "most mappings are simple". That misjudges that there is hardly any correlation between the number of mappings and the effort or complexity involved for delivering them. Each change to a mapping needs to be evaluated, described, coded, unit tested internally, validated externally, installed in a test environment, integration tested, and documented.

The truth is that there are few ways of significantly cutting down costs for an industrial-strength and enterprise-worthy and enterprise-ready solution: It is going to take 4 to 8 months, and it is going to take a number of skills and on average the equivalent of between 2 and 3 senior-level resources. This is because you need to profoundly re-design the out-of-the-box sample code (if you even use it, which I don't see a good reason for), use or develop additional ABAP and XSLT components, address and bake performance into the design early on, consider the technical and functional solution architecture, and because specifications are likely to take multiple iterations and some sort of prototype before they are close enough to be called finalized.

> **LEARNING.** Don't delay the project and spend your money on a lengthy effort to pick up some of the skills needed and to identify presumed shortcuts. Accept the functional, process and technical complexity of this solution, significantly reduce and almost eliminate all risk, get predictability and proven solutions. Use your effort to get a reasonable assurance of the quality of services, push for predictability and risk sharing, but do not cut key elements from a project plan or toolset.
>
> Your company's long-term budget will thank you for it.

Myth 4. "We know what we need"

This statement often is combined with a desire to cut short design efforts.

In reality almost all clients I have seen do only have a basic understanding of what they need, and even more rarely do they consider aspects that go beyond pure mapping functionality. Even in the best of situations such functionality is described under the assumption of a perfectly well-functioning technical environment, and without specific regard to data cleansing or data conversion efforts.

The truth is that validation of the scope and a distinct detailed design effort are essential to a successful implementation. It then even goes one step further, adding a further refinement and slight revision of specifications once the business had a chance to touch and feel a prototype.

Theory and 'Real' Design Work

Look at it this way. How much more difficult is it to theoretically come up with a design without the ability to see and touch it? Imagine the thought processes that needs to go into envisioning what each solution component looks like in each circumstance and how users will confront it, and then describing all this verbally. This is a monumental effort, and even in the best case it has natural limits.

Design involves users mocking up a solution and playing around with a product, addressing nuances, identifying shortcomings, and triggering odd and creative thought processes. The iPad was not drawn on a white board and then produced, it involved numerous iterations and refinements on every level.

It's the same with software, and I am a firm believer in seeing and touching being designing and believing. The most mature design specifications I have been confronted with were the result of a multi-year effort. This effort could have been cut short significantly by performing a condensed series of successively more involved reflections on the design, from a rough mockup without an actual interface, to a proof of concept (POC), a prototype, a unit tested near-perfect solution, to the confrontation with the real data and the real users in the real world out there.

Thinking of it, that is almost exactly what eventually happened anyway.

What the business team usually is good at is to describe a very high-level process flow, the generic object-level mappings, and many of the detailed mappings.

What is missing is almost always the consideration for:

- Technical complexities to optimize performance, and how performance optimization involves addressing

functional aspects. Just think of conditional updates, or status controls, or optional mappings.
- Transfer controls like starting and stopping a transfer, duplicate triggering of transfers (concurrency control), or the reprocessing of errors.
- Status management based on a complete project life cycle, like triggering the release of an object in SAP based on a UDF in Primavera, or the setting of a complete status in SAP and then Primavera.
- The impact of authorization controls in SAP and Primavera.
- Implications of the application landscape, e.g. locations of servers and performance of user transactions.
- Consequences of Primavera configuration and related limitations, e.g. resource rates, WBS IDs, field lengths, or calendars.
- User-friendly error handling and the system supporting the identification and resolution of errors or data inconsistencies.
- Challenges related to data conversion, like missing mappings of keys, inconsistent settings, duplication of records, or "dirty" data.
- Actual data and how that may lead to missing field entries, unexpected missing logic (e.g. forgetting to set a logical conditions for a rarely used control key), or require additional logic to be introduced for a splitting of data target systems, including authorizations and security.

"Know what we need" is also often limited to one-dimensional functional requirements. These rarely consider unit test or integration test scenarios that follow a project life cycle from various angles.

The above is not really a problem unless it is unexpected. In my experience it is impossible to define specifications of a complex process in advance. Narrowing down of requirements is a process that requires hands-on touching of a solution, and a gradual refinement, particularly when being confronted with actual data.

LEARNING. Keep in mind complexities derived from aspects like:

- Technical considerations
- Status management considerations
- Complete scenarios considering the whole project life cycle
- Error handling and support requirements
- Data conversion
- Usability for the end-user

Perform a formal workshop that helps validating scope, then a detailed design using a reference environment, then document, then review, then prototype, then unit test.

Consider that minor changes will be made until the last moment. The goal of an implementation is not to deliver on stated functionality but the most workable solution for the end user, within the general parameters defined at the outset.

Myth 5. "We need an EPC Consultant"

No you don't. You need a team, and the right team at that.

This statement goes hand-in-hand with "Just teach me" and "All I need", which I also frequently encounter.

Misperceptions.

More specifically, you need a number of specialized skills and people that understand enough of the other areas involved, so that all falls nicely in place. The statement about an EPC consultant usually comes from one of two misperceptions.

A. The first one is that this is equivalent to bringing on board a consultant for a specific module of SAP, like a PS consultant or a PM consultant. This keeps the focus on functionality but even then underestimates that one needs to deal with two different business applications, not just modules. It helps looking at SAP and Primavera as more different than the modules of SAP PS and PM.

B. The second one is that establishing an integrated schedule bridging SAP and Primavera is primarily a technical task. While this already is limiting by not considering functional aspects, the focus on technical aspects itself is not sufficient. Complete implementations require an understanding of SAP ABAP and some Basis System functions, of EPC XSLT skills and Primavera Java API skills.

Sometimes I hear clients say "we have ABAP skills in-house" or "we have PS expertise in-house" or "we have Primavera expertise in-house". That may very well be the case, and hopefully is. It still disregards the learning curve of the job at hand.

It Takes a Team

It also does not take into account that having a great variety of skills is a necessary but not sufficient condition to take on full ownership of the solution, or even to expand on it. What it requires is the coordination of these skills and making sure everybody understands their respective place and contribution. This requires experience and extensive communication, best acquired during the implementation of the SAP-Primavera integration solution itself.

Just consider the number of bi-directional links and relationships that need to be understood.

- If it is one module only, then one does just need to understand its capabilities.
- If it is SAP and Primavera, then there is one link, on top of two skills.
- If it is ABAP and XSLT, then there come two more skills and one link.
- Combining the last two renders four different skills and six different links.

- And then add Primavera Java API skills and you are at five distinct skills and the need to understand ten different links.

I am not trying to sell you that you need to hire five people and let them hang around for a year like it used to happen when implementing SAP. But asking for an EPC consultant is like asking for an ERP consultant to implement SAP ERP. Which one is it that you would like to have, the Basis consultant or the Controlling consultant or the Procurement consultant or the Human Resources consultant? I hope you get the picture.

LEARNING. Respect the high number of moving parts that you are trying to align, and that these involve a stark variety of skills.

Make sure you match external skills with internal ones to maximize know-how transfer, but don't expect this to be a fast process. I have seen impressive abilities of clients to support customized implementations even after we left. An example is Mark Morgan and his team at Eskom in South Africa. They were involved from the outset of the project, though, and did not replace but complement the external expertise.

Myth 6. "We need more time to decide"

Am I repeating myself? Again my answer is, "No, you don't." Follow the above-described three steps for picking a tool and move on.

In financial terms, the only logical argument justifying the delay of a decision would be if there were no tools or proven solutions out there. But there are! You can buy a complete solution of a tailored implementation, covering software and solutions, for a fixed price and a fixed implementation timeframe. Using tools from SAP and Oracle, otherwise platform independent. This is the case for 95%+ of all requirements I have ever seen.

Remember Your Cost-Benefit Analysis?

Above all, though, don't forget the first of all steps, knowing why you do it. You have a significant pain point. You did a cost benefit analysis. You want to get better at adapting and transforming your business. Do you really want to wait for anything but the most dramatic reasons?

I have seen several clients agonizing for years about how to best implement an integration. Sometimes they acknowledge that they are not ready, or that processes are not standardized enough yet.

Sometimes they are taken aback because of the money.

Take this case: Per the U.S. Energy Association (USEA), during a typical turnaround a petrochemical plant loses between $1 million and $4 million of revenue a day (let's call it $2 million), with an average outage time of between 20 and 60 days (let's call it 40 days), and costs of about $30 million to $50 million (let's call it $40 million, or $1 million per day).

Cut down the outage time by 5%, which is 2 days. You gain $4 million in revenue and greatly reduced costs. Your overall margins improve, you get savings, you have better data for your postmortems, can benchmark better, and you can analyze and improve.

Then tell me why again you delay a decision to a point where 5 or 6 turnarounds pass without you taking advantage of what is ready to be implemented?!

You could make a similar case about the savings of integrating contractor Primavera schedules into your Owner SAP PS schedules, and gaining related budget controls and earned value analysis capabilities. On a $1 billion-a-year capital project, resulting savings of 0.5% would be $5 million.

When delaying your decision, are you wasting colossal amounts of money, or are you just wasting significant amounts of money? It probably depends on your definition of "colossal" and "significant".

Either way a million bucks is a million bucks, and it sounds a lot to me not matter how you put it.

LEARNING. Treat the evaluation and decision-making process like a quick mini-project and save substantial amounts of money. Do this by assembling a team covering all required skills, express clear expectations, gather outside input as necessary, and perform a workshop whose results you document very well. All this should not take longer than several weeks.

Yes, you likely have to pay for some of the external services, but you are likely to save as much or more in cutting down internal costs, not to speak of opportunity costs. The outcome will be a working document that can act as a guideline to be included in a Statement of Work or Project Charter, or in an RFI.

Myth 7. "No Customization – No Coding"

"No Customization" - really?! Let me say this again - reeaallly?!

You implemented SAP, turned your business upside down for it, likely also implemented and used Primavera for a while. Are you now saying that implementing an interface to bridge these two complex applications should be done using a "one-size-fits-all" generic sample provided by the vendor of the integration platform?

In short, this is not going to happen. No way. There will be customization, and you really want customization, since that is what you have done to your business process also. The tool needs to adapt to the business needs, and only rarely should it be the other way around.

In SAP EPC, configuration of mappings and logic even is done through code. There is no pretense of putting some cool but limiting interface in the middle to make it "look better". For many or even most cases modifications involve XSLT changes, although often ABAP code may also be required in many instances, and rarely also Java.

This is no issue, though. Like with configuration of the Implementation Guide in SAP ECC, using XSLT to customize logic in EPC is straightforward and can in theory be done quickly. It's just that, also like configuration in SAP ECC, the thought process, the mocking up of the solution, the documentation, the testing and then refining of the solution can take a substantial amount of time. Well-justified time, that is.

And sometimes it is much more complex than that. If fields are missing, and the API needs to be enhanced, or if performance needs to be optimized, conditional updates introduced, or code needs to be refactored to simplify support - this may involve ABAP and more elaborate coding efforts. If that solves a business issue and enhances the overall solution, though, then it should be justified.

Think of EPC more like the iPad or iPhone of the business user. No, of course it isn't, but consider the following analogy: Without apps, how powerful would these tools be? They would be okay, but they wouldn't be what extends "me" and makes me as productive as can be. In a similar way, a number of extensions, add-ons, features, functions, enhancements and advanced templates greatly extend the value one gets from the EPC platform itself.

Since we understand the often negative connotation of the word "coding", we call it "tailoring". This is not the same as putting lipstick on a pig, more like putting makeup on Julia Roberts or a face-mask on Tom Cruise - it's still a beauty one way or doesn't matter the other.

LEARNING. Liberate yourself from the pretentious "no coding" paradigm and embrace functionality, as long as modifications follow approaches formally endorsed by SAP Labs, the owners of their EPC product. In my business we have put several man-years of R&D efforts into developing solution components and implementation accelerators. This is not hacked code, but these are well-structured, well-built and well-documented capabilities that greatly enhance the overall solution, reduce risk, are tested and proven, and get the job done very well.

Don't throw away the benefits of that. Any solution on the market would at least have to provide the same, no matter what platform they use. Or how do you think anybody else "tailors" their solutions to customer's requirements? Using music? Or using code? Okay, now I am really trying to be funny. But the fact is that it's all there with EPC, so get over words like "customization" or "code".

Myth 8. "Our IT can handle this"

This statement almost always reflects an incorrect view of the nature of SAP-Primavera integration, by putting it in the realm of a technical challenge to be resolved by technical people. Yes, in principle smart and skilled people can figure it out, but at what cost, at what timeline, what risk, and what quality?

It is the nature of most enterprise organizations that I encounter to have strong and capable information technology departments. Often I then see these IT departments tasked with evaluating integration tools, immediately jumping to Step 3 of the process. Then they are tasked with implementing a software tool.

It does not have to be that way, although under certain conditions this is do-able. IT may purely manage the project, and take all the right steps. Or they really happen to have the right people in place, and experience on top of that. More often than not, however, this is not the case. It almost never is the case with SAP-Primavera integration because this is such a rarely performed and specialized effort in any market.

The reality is that typically (a) IT does not know, (b) IT cannot know, and (c) IT should not even have to know.

IT does not know.

"Our IT knows what to do". Yeah right. How often have they been integrating SAP with Primavera? And keep in mind that this is a no-win question: If they have been doing it many times, their success rate (and competency?) could be questioned. If they have not done it before, how could they possibly know how to tackle one of the most complex task of the enterprise business application world?

IT cannot know.

The world is complex. There are hundreds of software tools and technologies out there, plus hardware, networks, databases, and much more. IT deals with security, authentication and authorizations, operating systems, productivity tools, standard business applications, etc. etc. etc.

How could they do a stellar job in something as esoteric as integrating Primavera and SAP? Is everybody a genius nowadays? And can every genius follow something as seemingly warped as business logic produced by SAP and Oracle? Gimme rockets science or the relativity theory, sometimes. Or why do you need to put a "T" instead of a "D" in a setting to make sure a field is called "Day"?

IT does not have to know.

Above all, as mentioned above over and over again, IT plays a critical role enabling the solution. Inherently, though, the pain point is a business one, and the solution delivery should be driven by the business also. It is highly questionable whether it makes sense to build full-fledged expertise in what is likely to be rarely required skills. For example, keeping some Primavera API or EPC installation or XSLT or ABAP experience in-house is very valuable. After all, IT should be able to support the solution after Go Live. However, this is a far cry from having to know all the intricacies of all the moving parts of a business solution that follows complex rules.

LEARNING. In almost all circumstances IT does not know, cannot know, and even if they would know they are usually the wrong people to drive this project in the first place. There is no issue with using IT to manage the project, if that is a role they are capable of performing in such a complex environment. But don't use them as the driver, and don't assume that they have sufficient internal skills and experience to deliver the project.

Bonus Features.
TECHNICAL PITFALLS

#1. Addressing Performance Too Late

The Problem: Addressing performance too late and therefore not delivering it

Here we are talking, to speak in the words of Angus Scott-Knight, about the difference between drinking a cup of tea versus playing a round of golf.

Instantaneous updates ("it is in SAP the moment I save in Primavera") are only theoretically possible, and upon deeper reflection not even preferred. Reports could become meaningless since they would be using moving targets where individual data aspects have been updated (e.g. completion or dates) while directly corresponding items may not have cleared all process hurdles (e.g. approval of actual hour confirmations).

This ominous "P" word, as I have heard an SAP Labs expert once call it, becomes a challenge because the alternative to the above is to synchronize a large number of objects periodically. It could be something like a daily or twice daily synchronization of

20,000 activities between SAP and Primavera, or the synchronization of 80,000 activities per week-end for just one large capital project.

A strategy that usually works for a while, but only for some project team members, is to disregard performance, keep the head in the sand until after functionality-focused integration test cycles, then declare victory, and hand it on to support. I say this strategy works, but of course only for the ones who get out quickly enough so that the "techies" and the support staff, or the usual culprits SAP or Oracle can get the blame. For whoever gets out quickly enough, the project can count as a success and another feather is in the cap...

It does not work for the users, though, and can even make a solution unworkable. Frustrations mount up, and the look for some other "interface" starts up again.

All this can be prevented. The key to it is to address it upfront.

There are smart ways of delivering very acceptable performance levels, with tens of thousands of activities synchronized in a matter of minutes. One of my rules of thumb is that the dimension of 1000 activities per minute are achievable. This gives us a starting point.

Maximizing performance is only to a degree a matter of hardware or software, but much more so one of using the right processes, logic and tools, and of using them the right way.

It starts with defining the system landscape with performance in mind. Keep the servers close to each other, on the same network. Put the various components on servers that are appropriately powered. Above all, though: Update smartly!

Only changes need to be brought over. This needs to be incorporated into the design from the beginning. Only changes should be updated, which is a task that out-of-the-box EPC does not inherently deliver. One needs to implement the capability for conditional updates, e.g. don't overwrite each field each time, apply only changes. At CEI we have built a conditional updates engine as part of our enhancement pack, and we are using it every single time.

You get the big bang for your performance buck when you limit the data volume that you are touching in the first place. This can dramatically improve performance by a dimension or two. We are talking possibly about synchronizing 15,000 activities in 10 minutes, instead of 500!

Then you go deeper into the field level conditional updates, then you optimize batch sizes and number of threads (EPC supports multi-threading), identify bottleneck after bottleneck, and remove it.

Whatever you do, though, hopefully you do not start approaching performance as an afterthought!

Here is a (incomplete) list of aspects to consider when trying to improve performance.

- Limiting the data volume
- Conditional updates
- System and application landscape
- Batch sizes
- Number of threads
- Power of servers (RAM)
- Bandwidth
- Transfer scheduling
- Database optimization
- Limitation of field mappings (e.g. no duplications on several levels)
- Smart logic in the XSLT
- Limiting number of API calls
- Incorporate additional logic into ABAP API
- Direct access to database tables ("last resort" and for read only transactions)

As usual, the solutions are all supported or even made possible by this oh-so-powerful EPC platform. It just is not part of the out-of-the-box solution, which is not more than an example. The following screen print depicts part of a proven solution. Using the accumulated knowledge of years of software engineering, and considering learnings from our past dozen or so SAP-Primavera implementations, the technical team at CEI has built a complete toolset to support performance optimization, called Transfer Manager.

How to Prevent the Pitfall:

- Address performance early, baking performance optimization into the original design
- Consider performance in very design decision
- Limit the number of data to be transferred, thus limiting costly API calls
- Look at the whole range of factors impacting performance - they add up

#2. Trusting Out-of-the-Box Mappings Too Much

The Problem: Putting too much trust into the out-of-the-box templates, and trying to stick too closely to it

The SAP-provided template does not reflect best practices or even proven practices. It does not really claim to do so (anymore...). Rather it provides a maximum number of mappings using standard BAPIs, roughly mimicking one almost a decade old live implementation.

This is a far cry from offering ready-to-deploy templates that reflect mature processes.

Just consider that the scenarios are PM and PS scenarios. PM and PS does not say much about the process and business challenge to be resolved. In PM, are we talking about Turnaround Management based on revisions, or Routine Maintenance schedules based on projects or functional locations? Or about a high number of Outages of a linear asset like a railroad? And what about the capital (= PS) work done during such Outages?

I even dare saying that one should read between the lines when SAP Labs makes informal statements about how easy it is to make mapping changes and how fast implementations therefore can go. At a utility in Houston, Texas, an initial estimate of client project management was "9 days", based on input from SAP and by interpreting the SAP's (then) web page claim of how quick implementation could be.

The actual effort was far beyond 100 days, with not one hour of wasted time. Rather, the client was so excited about the level of commitment and quality of work delivered that the project manager said to me, paraphrased, "This has been the most professional delivery of services I have ever seen."

This is not about the capabilities of the EPC platform. Those can hardly be exaggerated. But it is about using the examples. Just because it is "easy to change" does not mean changing 80 individual mappings, adding status-dependent logic throughout the life-cycle, performance enhance the whole bunch, provide advanced error handling on top of the logic, consider real data - that all of that is a snap to design, document, prototype, test, fix, retest, train and support.

How to Prevent the Pitfall:

- Consider the out-of-the-box EPC template only as a general reference to familiarize yourself with the basic mechanisms of the platform, and how the various moving parts interact with each other.
- Stay posted for when advanced templates have reached a stage of "rapid deployment functionality". Some of those out there are already quite close. Just don't assume that this would shave off more than half the costs for implementation services. There still is a lot to do.
- Do what you have to do to deliver the functionality the business needs. Don't skimp out. If your business case urges you to deliver something half-baked very fast, revisit Step 1 of the implementation steps, or just don't do the project.

#3. Keeping Error Handling Too Technical

The Problem: Considering the default error logs as sufficient for support

Like other platforms EPC comes with elaborate error logs. The tool generates thousands of lines of log entries that document in detail what happened during transfers. These entries contain standard technical error messages from SAP and Primavera, have date and time stamps, and lots of details about the data moved and logic applied.

What they don't have is a description of what the problem is. The default app does not know what logic the tailored app tried to apply. Cryptic error messages do not help a user to figure out what he or she did wrong.

Like with most business applications, most "errors" are operating errors, failure to follow the right steps, or unexpected and invalid data. In other words it is the failure to follow the specific logical assumptions that are technically reflected in the solution.

For the most frequent or likely inconsistencies and errors, such specifics are to be found out and communicated as clearly as possible to the user. Standard messages are too general. They cannot know what and why a certain behavior or action is expected for a specific logic. One of the worst cases may even be if the solution updates Primavera and no error or warning messages are shown even though they should be.

For example, if the system were to say "invalid resource ID" this would be meaningless, but if it were to say "Work center ELEC01 on Activity 3065 of Network 600000067 has the status 'locked' in SAP and cannot be used", a user could self-correct this. Or if an activity has been set to status "deletion flag" in SAP, a message in the transfer report may point out that "Activity 4010 of Network 600004580 is not updated because it has been deleted in SAP".

Even more, by running an upfront simulation, such mistakes could have been caught and prevented even before trying the actual update and data transfer.

A user cannot be expected to sift through thousands of lines of log entries. Even support personnel should not have to do that for the overwhelming majority of issues. Spending a reasonable amount of time and effort, maybe even just a few days, on tuning error handling can be one of the highest-value steps toward user-acceptance of the overall solution.

How to Prevent the Pitfall:

- Review the specific business logic to be defined during the detailed design and translate typical violations of the logic into meaningful error or warning messages that a user can self-diagnose, interpret, and correct.
- Consider adding the ability to run simulations of transfers so that issues can be caught before the actual transfer.
- Empower end-users by informing them about logical behavior that is to be expected, turning issues into an opportunity to increase acceptance of the solution.

#4. Undervaluing Transfer Admin Functions

The Problem: Inability to interfere with or tune the default transfer transaction

Being able to control transfers is another aspect closely related to user acceptance, since it can help bypassing highly frustrating situations, eliminate performance issues, and even prevent data integrity issues. A look at some examples shows these possible sources of issues and irritations.

When you start the default EPC transaction, it will run as is, in its totality. There is no way to stop it, and then start again.

There is no way to reprocess errors only. No way to see performance statistics so that you can react and tune batch sizes or number of threads. All these can be particularly frustrating in production, and when dealing with large data volumes. Potentially it could even render the transaction unworkable.

You have no ability to abandon the whole lot and start again. If you reprocess you will not just trigger a second transfer but that one may in rare circumstances even conflict with the first one and lead to concurrency and therefore data integrity issues.

Add the issues described above, relating to error handling and performance, and you have a potential perfect storm of user frustrations ready to boil over and declare that EPC comes with severe limitations.

No it does not. It just is that the out-of-the-box example does not address these aspects. But there are solutions on the market. Our team at CEI has successfully addressed all the above issues and challenges.

With such enhancements and add-ons, users are empowered and their acceptance and satisfaction is greatly improved, support issues are minimized, and technical inconsistencies are eliminated. All of this uses the powerful EPC platform and recommended ways of extending the example solution.

How to Prevent the Pitfall:

- Don't misjudge the value of user satisfaction and the opportunity to empower users.
- Use proven enhancements and add-ons from the EPC partner ecosystem to introduce detailed transfer controls. Combine them with performance enhancement tools and advanced custom error handling, and people are tuning the solution instead of being tuned by it.

Bonus Features.
FUNCTIONAL PITFALLS

#5. Overextending Primavera's Resource Management

The Problem: Pushing too much resources functionality to Primavera.

Maximizing Primavera's strong resources management capabilities is certainly an understandable goal. Trying to do too much, and in the wrong way, can cause more issues than benefits, though.

Let's start with the non-contentious one. Transferring SAP work centers as resource assignments while creating them in the Primavera resource library is straightforward. It provides visibility into SAP plans. Primavera can then use this input to optimize resource availability, at least to some degree.

Then things are getting a bit more challenging, with three arguments and wishes I keep hearing about:

1.   I want to assign skill-based resources (or roles) to activities in Primavera.

2.   I want to assign individual resources to activities in Primavera.

3.   I want to pull resource cost rates into Primavera.

The underlying scheme is the vision of performing "resource-loaded scheduling" in Primavera. The reality is that while this is in theory not impossible, hardly anyone tries or achieves this anyway. All too often reality gets in the way.

Above all, Primavera does not have an HR module. It can address labor, non-labor, or material resources, can structure them according to (one) hierarchy, group them according to user-defined fields, and assign them to roles. Not really more. So one can get cool graphs, and they are meaningful to a degree. What do they reflect, though?

Work calendars in Primavera can change, but are they mapped to a localized holiday calendar, considering public holidays and individual vacation? What about time off as reflected in a human resources application? SAP typically has all this data and capabilities, at least it can have it if it is configured, set up, and consistently maintained.

This is not to say that SAP is the way to go here, although they offer their own "solution" called Multi-Resource Scheduling (MRS). It integrates the assignment of resources with their availability and qualifications. In theory this is the most powerful resource assignment tool. In reality it is over-engineered. The fact that one needs a huge screen to fit the various pieces of information together is just a symptom.

The deeper issue is that this whole function is very complex and top-down heavy and engineering-centric. That is not just MRS, but trying to do what MRS tries to do, and what the above three points try to insinuate many users want to do in Primavera.

I see the long-term solution as substantially different. The assignment should stick to basic trades or skills or roles, and leave the individual resource assignment to team leads or gang leads or work center managers, or whatever the title is. They know not just what is on paper, but what their people are really like.

Working with resources, including assigning them, is a task of humans. This cannot really be managed top-down, as a study of networks and complex systems would quickly confirm. The more efficient approach is to leave the assignment and optimization as low to the people on the ground (foremen, managers) as possible, who know the individuals and can make judgment calls that a system or a removed scheduler simply cannot.

Back to the above three points. They all can be done, although they gradually increase complexity of the integration solution. The first one will require to synchronize the complete resources library every time a transfer runs. The second one needs to extend this to HR resource assignments, including updates of the resources hierarchy. The third one requires the pulling of standard cost rates from SAP into Primavera, including the alignment of processes.

Don't bite off more than you can digest, though, and check up on complexity and networks theory. You may come to the same conclusion as I did, that decentralized actions and the use of mobile applications can resolve the assignment of individual resources more efficiently than 19th and 20th century style top-down and hierarchy-based planning approaches ever could.

How to Prevent the Pitfall:

- In Primavera, start by sticking to the assignment of work centers, skills, or roles, whether from SAP or in Primavera. Only slowly expand on that capability, once a clear benefit has been proven.
- Be aware that assigning of resources in Primavera can inherently not consider all information and will therefore not be optimized.
- Consider alternative ways of assigning individuals, led by team leads and using mobile tools.

#6. Underestimating the Impact of Defining Projects

The Problem: Underestimating the impact of defining Primavera projects and related selections of orders or activities

One of the powerful capabilities of SAP EPC is the ability mix and match objects in a non-intuitive manner. It enables you to reflect substantially different mappings on an object level. Most extremely this can be seen in the many variations in which turnaround and outage projects are defined.

Here is what I have seen: A utility in Brisbane, Australia, defines outages by an individual WBS element of a PS project. A nuclear utility in South Africa maps a revision to a project. A utility in the U.S. looks at combinations of functional locations and plants. A chemical corporation uses a combination of PS Project, PM Revision and Location to group work orders by Primavera project. A refinery in the U.S. uses the time horizon to move work orders between routine maintenance windows. A railroad in Australia uses multiple revision codes so that orders can dynamically be moved between different Primavera projects.

This is another instance where the out-of-the-box functionality is grossly simplistic. Let's assume the highest level mapping is of one SAP Revision to one Primavera Project. If somebody now selects a wider range of orders in SAP than belong to the revision, how should the system react? Should a partial update of another project happen? Should certain orders be ignored?

Furthermore, what happens if somebody removes an order in SAP from a revision or project? Or in Primavera? Either one could happen by mistake, or on purpose. Either one could affect the schedule. The overall goal is to find exactly those orders that are managed together in Primavera. That is tricky but do-able, just not with the out-of-the-box sample mappings.

The scalability of EPC allows to address even more complex scenarios, like selecting orders associated with multiple revisions, assigning them to a single Primavera project, and grouping them to review scope and budget changes.

How to Prevent the Pitfall:

- Be very clear about the highest-level mapping. Add additional logic if helpful.
- Include "missing order" or "missing activity" and discrepancy reports that inform the scheduler when inconsistencies occur.
- Exclude the majority of selections from the out-of-the-box selection screen, to ensure data integrity and prevent discrepancies to occur in the first place.
- Provide meaningful error messages so that users can interpret issues, like objects deleted in SAP.

#7. Misjudging the Complexity of Integrating Scheduled Dates

The Problem: Misjudging the complexity of integrating calendars and scheduling parameters

It is simple, right? Primavera scheduling calculates dates and EPC updates SAP constraints, correct? Not necessarily.

The devil is in the details. Obviously planners and schedulers in Primavera need to be able to condense schedules, change relationships, and assign more resources to get a job done faster. That is part of the deal and a main reason for the integration in the first place. Actions in SAP may impact the schedule also, though, and schedulers need to know about this in Primavera, ideally without their actions getting overwritten.

However, keep in mind that the ability to schedule in SAP should be turned off, e.g. through the setting of status DSEX (Dates Scheduled Externally). SAP configuration may also help to prevent conflicts between SAP and Primavera calculations.

Actuals posted in SAP may need to set a started status and start dates being in Primavera, for example, and changes in the numbers of resources assigned may impact the schedule. In some cases feedback of procurement dates may need to feed back into the schedule, and constraints - or reference dates - may be pushed down from SAP sales orders or SAP milestones or SAP WBS elements.

The above can be aggravated depending on the specific scheduling parameters used in Primavera. Actual hours coming from SAP may then impact completion information or calculation of scheduled dates. Half a dozen parameters can affect the scheduling of dates, like activity type, duration type, % complete type, or the activity calendar on the Primavera activity, or Units/Time and remaining hours on the resource assignment.

Therefore, even if there is an "in principle" strict division of responsibilities between SAP and Primavera, depending on what application performs what aspect of such changes, this can impact data in the respective other one.

How to Prevent the Pitfall:

When designing the solution, do not just focus on straightforward mappings. Validate and refine these mappings and the related logic by walking through the project life-cycle while focusing on aspects of time management. Review complete processes throughout all relevant dynamics, not just stationary mappings of fields.

#8. Underestimating the Complexity of Status Management

The Problem: Underestimating the complexity of status management across SAP and Primavera

Which one is the system of record? It is SAP, isn't it? Who owns the data? It is both SAP and Primavera, correct? Or not? The short answer is that it depends on the overall process, and since managing a project is among the most complex processes in any business application, the specifics of the answer are not always straightforward. They are definitely more complex than a simple mapping of similar fields.

A frequent question I hear from customers is about who owns the data. This is a typical example of where generic mappings are not enough. To give the correct answer one needs to consider the project life cycle, in general and for each object. This introduces breakpoints and changes of ownership in the overall life-cycle, but potentially also for each individual objects, like an activity.

When you plan in SAP, as is typical for maintenance-related activities, introduce a status to authorize the respective activity to be scheduled in Primavera. That may not authorize work on that activity yet, since financially relevant transactions may need to be released. Such a release may require the setting of another status in SAP, and updating of a user-defined field or code in Primavera to inform the scheduler that the activity is ready to go.

Once work on an activity has started, you may introduce status changes in either application. There needs to be clarity about it, though, to prevent surprising scheduling results. For example, when time has been posted in SAP, an activity should be considered started in Primavera also.

If Primavera controls the reporting of progress completion, the completion of 100% of the work may need to update SAP. However, one needs to consider that statuses in SAP may restrict postings of financials. Therefore there needs to be some logical consideration to not prevent late postings to be charged to an object.

Other status-related questions make this even less straightforward. What happens if somebody in SAP locks an activity and does not allow actual postings against it anymore? Should that finish it? Or what if an activity or operation in SAP is deleted?

A very Primavera-centric solution I have seen controlled the release of activities in SAP using triggers in Primavera. This may make sense, but there is a hurdle: There are less stringent and less detailed authorization controls in Primavera than in SAP. Does finance in SAP really not mind if a Primavera scheduler determines when actual postings to an activity are allowed or not?

The question of status can even extend to other areas and introduce additional complexities:

- Resources.
  What should happen in Primavera if a resource (i.e. a work center or individual HR record) is not active anymore?
- Revision.
  What should happen in Primavera if a revision is not active but work orders are associated with them?
- Projects in the maintenance world.
  What happens if the status of a project or WBS element changes even though maintenance work orders are attached to it?

How to Prevent the Pitfall:

Acknowledge that detailed design is about much more than a generic mapping of fields. Walk through a project life cycle step by step, for each object, to determine the handing off of ownership from one application to another one. Do this multiple times, using a different perspective each time, like progressing an activity, or the calculation of dates, or the planning of hours and posting of actuals. Pay particular attention to the interaction between Start and Finish in Primavera, and REL, TECO, and CLSD in SAP.

#9. Trying to Manage Costs in Primavera

The Problem: Trying to push too much cost functionality to Primavera

As an ERP system, SAP has strong cost and financials management capabilities. Primavera inherently does not. That should almost close out the topic. It is difficult to make general statements beyond this, since specific industries and specific processes vary so much. The answer may differ, e.g., depending on whether one manages turnarounds, internal R&D efforts, or capital projects.

As a rule of thumb, though, do challenge the value of bringing cost data from a powerful cost management application to a scheduling application. Violating that rule of thumb is likely to introduce complexity, while still missing key targets.

A high-level walk through key types of costs shows the complexity of the picture, and Primavera's limitations to deal with it:

- Budgets.
  This is the SAP terminology of approved cost buckets that authorize spending. Typically budgets are established through a corporate bottom-up and top-down budgeting process, resulting in authorizing funds by project or by a high-level SAP WBS structure that reflects a cost breakdown structure (CBS). They inherently originate in SAP, and if for the pure reason that Primavera does not have some workflow and approval controls for cost budgets.

- Cost plans.
  This is the SAP terminology for detailed bottom-up plans incorporating labor cost, material cost, and a variety of overhead allocations. Such plans inherently originate in SAP, and can have a large number of sources. Primavera would only approximately be able to simulate as a rough version of such a plan, and even then definitely without considering overhead or other allocations. Any development of a version of such a plan would be greatly simplified, e.g. due to the lacking ability of Primavera to incorporate negotiated or calculated rates for materials or externally procured services.

- Commitments and other Procurement Data.
  In SAP terminology, commitments are the equivalent of purchase requisitions or even purchase orders, before goods or service have been received and turned into actuals. The origin of this information can only be in SAP

since this is where the procurement application is. The total committed amounts may at time be a helpful reference to be transferred into Primavera, should schedulers need to consider cost data in their work.

- Labor Cost Rates.
SAP has the ability to determine standard labor cost rates through multiple means, and to associate a virtually unlimited number of rates with resources. Primavera can only keep five rates per resource. Here you quickly can reach limits when considering regular and various kinds of overtime cost rates, particularly when linking them to work calendars and different kinds of services that may be provided by a resource.

- Actuals Costs.
Since this is where financial accounts are affected, actual costs have to end up in SAP, and in almost all cases they originate there. This applies to the specific hours multiplied by hourly cost rates provided by internal or external labor resources, to materials procured, to overhead allocations, or internally produced materials. Even one of the most useful data elements in Primavera, actual hours of time worked, is typically captured using the SAP CATS module.

I have seen a large Canadian Oil & Gas company and a major European Engineering company replicate cost rates from SAP into Primavera. I also have seen another large Canadian Oil & Gas company pull data out of Primavera (partly put there through an interface to SAP) to create elaborate earned value calculations. To enable time-phased cash flow calculations, I have also noticed attempts of a premier supplier of the nuclear power industry to pull cost related data into Primavera. Neither one of these attempts has convinced me to change my basic opinion about the relatively small value considering to the vagueness and complexity of the related effort.

Use the strengths of each product, and don't try to replicate functionality.

Often the transfer of cost data from SAP is driven by an attempt to calculate earned value in Primavera. As noble of a goal as this seems, and even considering that Primavera's founder Joel Koppelman "wrote the book" on Earned Value, Primavera's earned value capabilities are not really superior to SAP's. Since a big part of SAP's job is to keep track of and post all cost information, this is the place to find the high-level budgets, contractual obligations, commitments, external procurement data, and actuals in real time.

What I see happen in almost all cases is that successful solutions provide Earned Value calculations out of SAP, often through extensions like Dassian to be compliant with industry-specific Earned Value standards, or out of Excel.

How to Prevent the Pitfall.

As a general rule:

- Limit cost integration to the pulling of data from SAP into Primavera.
- Limit cost integration to the pulling of summary information of budgets and general cost plans.
- Consider pulling actual rates from SAP, including revenues, but consider working with
- Do not try to replicate cost allocations managed in SAP, as overhead.
- Do not try to duplicate cost accounts from SAP into Primavera to perform bottom-up cost planning.
- Use cost data from SAP as references only.
- Focus on Primavera's strengths, i.e. calculations of dates, planned hours, and progress.

Bonus Features.

PROJECT MANAGEMENT PITFALLS

#10. Underestimating the Impact on End Users

The Problem: Disregarding requirements that affect end users

Does the following statement sound logical to you? "I understand that this is more than an installed interface, but it still is a primarily technical solution, running in the background with minimum impact on the end user." If you agree, think again, after reading some of the below points.

Yes, the integration product itself should ideally not have to be used by the end user when conducting their daily job. The transfers themselves should normally be scheduled, not manually triggered. The essence of the integration is then that users of SAP and users of Primavera both have better information available, faster, more reliably and more correct, while otherwise just doing their job using the tools as usual.

This assumes a perfect world and the absence of any issues. It also misses part of the point altogether. Underestimating the user primarily comes in three flavors:

1. Transfer logic can affect their job. Transfers should empower users, but not indiscriminately overwrite data that they have maintained manually. Sometimes data requires a human decision. For example, status changes may not supposed to happen automatically, or date constraints or changes of resource assignments or even descriptions should not be overwritten.

Let the user find out what has been added by setting indicators in Primavera. Display information in question as reference information and not by overwriting fields. You may even consider loading new data into a different EPS structure, or associate it with a separate WBS element. That way a scheduler has to touch it manually and work with it, as is his or her job in the first place.

2. Issues may be unclear to them. As much as we want to avoid it, errors and issues happen. Like with any other piece of technology, the handling of such errors can be an opportunity to gain credibility and trust, or to lose both. Therefore I urge you to make errors and warnings meaningful and descriptive.

It does not stop with their identification, though. Now also enable the user to make manual adjustments. This is particularly important for data conversion activities.

3. Not considering technical issues that may happen. A range of technical issues can happen if not properly addressed in the design and implementation of the solution. Consider performance or data integrity, or the ability to process errors. Make sure your solution has concurrency controls so that data can be trusted 100%.

Speed up transfers (performance!), enable error-only processing, and provide controls that do not leave the users helpless when the wrong button is pressed, like an "execute" with the wrong selection. Give them the ability to stop and start transfers, or process errors only. Consider one activity that may have been locked due to somebody else using it, or an issue with one field of 12,000 activities. Don't let the user wait "forever" to address such a small thing.

How to Prevent the Pitfall:

Involve business users early on. The solution design should allow touch-and-feel opportunities to end-users, like the playback of requirements through a prototype. Extend this involvement to the design of solution components in Primavera and SAP, e.g. as reports. Independent of the specific design, in general consider conditional updates, performance optimization, custom error-handling, transfer controls, and transfer simulations, one way or another.

#11. Unrealistic Timeframes

The Problem: Setting   of   and   pushing   for   unrealistic timeframes

Do you know you can watch a 100-minute movie in 12.5 minutes if you fast-forward it at 8 times the normal speed? And play a 16-hour audio book during a one-hour drive from Sarasota to Tampa in Florida, if you run it 16 times as fast as normal? Sure, you would not get much, or anything, out of it, but you can do it.

I guess it would be a similar effect if one tried just to fast forward the implementation of an SAP-Primavera integration solution. Here is how to ruin such an implementation:

1.   Declare that you know what you want by creating a mapping spreadsheet based on the out-of-the-box example mappings listed on SAP's web site. Then skip the scope validation and design phases.
2.   Install the out-of-the-box software somehow, with as much help from SAP Labs as possible.
3.   Hire somebody who has some XSL experience, possibly even a developer or support person from SAP.
4.   Make a few modifications to the standard mappings so that defaults point at (some of) your data.

5.   See data being pushed from SAP to Primavera.
6.   Declare success, laugh about the other idiots, and move on.

And then let me show you how to learn twice as much by listening to 2 audio books on my drive from Sarasota to Tampa, by fast-forwarding at 32 times the speed.

Would you really base your time estimate at something as nonsensical as I describe above? Of course not, but sometimes I feel like I am asked to argue about it!

No, unrealistic timeframes lead to pressures for dropping important implementation steps, such as:

- Eliminating detailed design and cutting down functionality.
- Dropping Prototyping.
- Cutting short testing.
- Not addressing change management.
- Disregarding the end user.
- Breaking processes instead of enhancing them.
- Leaving solutions dysfunctional by keeping them slow.
- Risking data integrity issues.
- Tackling real-life data too late.
- And so many more.

One would not do anything like that to an arguably more straightforward implementation of SAP PS and IM, or PPM, or even when writing a bunch of custom reports.

Why am I even talking about it? Because I keep encountering such notions out there in the market place! Even when millions of dollars of value for each project are affected, or the ability to effectively execute a business strategy.

How to prevent the Pitfall:

Take your SAP-Primavera integration project serious. Remind yourself what enterprise projects are for, and how they add to the bottom-line. Stay aware that this is not a technical installation task, and that a single set of example mappings cannot even scratch the surface of what needs to be done. Demand high performance, attention to detail, user-friendliness, high quality, state-of-the-art processes, and do not take "no" for an answer. Don't compromise but do it right the first time.

#12. Acting Like a 'Milking Cow'

The Problem: Requesting so much input, demos and information from so many sources that one feels overly comfortable implementing a good solution without formal external help

This is a known phenomenon in the consulting world. A prospective client keeps dangling a carrot in front of everybody's nose, but has a hidden agenda of potentially doing it cheap, compromising quality of the solution, and just get something implemented. I call such behavior a "milking cow" since it somehow looks like a defense mechanism against having been "milked" by consultants one time too often.

It hits honest and trusting consultants with the most know-how the hardest, since they have most to give. The by far biggest loser is the prospective client, though.

I trace the possibility for this behavior down not as much to deliberate mischief, but to a combination of false advertising, sales talk by software vendors, and gross misjudgment of the facts that I outlined above in my Steps 2 to 6. Above all, though, it starts with not tending properly to the above Step 1. It reflects missing a dramatic value opportunity by focusing on a technocratic or functional approach instead one of strategy.

Implementing a SAP-Primavera integration solution can improve your project management maturity to a degree that turns it into one of the most crucial steps toward staying competitive. It is about an organization's ability to adapt to changing market conditions, achieve significant cost savings and efficiency gains, and in short to effectively and efficiently execute strategic business objectives that have been quantified and chosen in a portfolio management process.

Why would one want to take shortcuts, why would one not use the best tools, why would one not use the best people and approach and methodologies and experience and skills - if it can help the arguably most critical ability to survive and prosper in a market? It can only be due to a misjudgment of the context.

How to prevent the Pitfall:

Back to Square 1 - or rather Step 1. Remind yourself that you are about to integrate complex applications from SAP and Oracle. Keep in mind that virtually all change in organizations is initiated and executed through projects. And acknowledge that superior ability to execute is what may very well differentiate yourself from the rest of the pack.

No shortcuts, no milking of consultants. Know why you do it, set realistic parameters, pick the right tool, find the right people, design the right solution, and implement smartly. Then reap the benefits.

#13. Forgetting about Data Conversion

The Problem: Erroneously assuming that already started projects would be straightforward to convert using a standard solution process

The typical solution assumes a "clean" project start, usually in SAP based on the approval of a project through a portfolio management process or sales-related trigger and subsequent assignment of a budget. Then the project structure is gradually expanded in either application, statuses are changed, completion is reported, and actuals are incorporated in the process. This ensures that project objects like WBS elements and activities or milestones have keys that map them between SAP and Primavera.

But when a project has already started before the technical integration solution is put in place, several things will be missing. Most importantly there is no association between structural objects in Primavera and in SAP. These need to be manually established. The same is true for any other data that a normal process affects, like the above-mentioned statuses, actual data, or completion information.

An integration application may be able to help in setting up some of these relationships, though. With a reasonable effort it should be possible to define additional transfers that create detailed project structures that otherwise do not yet exist in either one of the applications. All you would need is a high-level association, e.g. of WBS elements.

This depends on the details, though. If in SAP already actuals have been posted, these are difficult to repost, and one would lose a big portion of their history. If similar but different objects already exist in both applications, mapping will need to be done manually. In short, it warrants a detailed analysis.

Consider baking in data structures and capabilities that support conversion activities. The main component is to base mappings on custom fields that can be manipulated manually by users. If you combine this with transfer simulations, enhanced transfer reports and custom error handling, the team gets a full set of tools to map data properly and bring it up to a state that enables the regular transfers to take over.

Data conversion may even be more complicated if Primavera itself is updated, or consolidated. That leads to a multi-step conversion effort, with Primavera data conversion first to be addressed.

How to Prevent the Pitfall:

Treat data conversion as a separate but related effort. If you know early on that it is in scope, ensure that field mappings, custom reporting, and custom error reporting all consider this effort. Done properly, this will enable end users to make manual adjustments if there are data issues.

#14. Underestimating Delays Due to Procurement Logistics

The Problem: Underestimating project procurement logistics

During my first SAP-Primavera Integration project using SAP EPC, in the beautiful city of Sydney in Australia, our team was affected big time by this pitfall. It ended up costing us hundreds of thousands of dollars in a fixed price project, and the personal stress level could hardly have been higher.

What happened? As we discovered too late, many critical project tasks were provided by contractors, and interests were not aligned. We needed more hard drive disk space, and the project was interrupted by more than two months (!) to follow proper corporate procurement processes. We needed to install the integration platform on another server, here came another resource from yet another vendor who needed to be trained up (again). Functional questions in Primavera needed to be answered, and there was another delay. We needed test data, encore.

Everybody else was working on a time and expense basis, while we had to retrain people, install software again, shift focus, re-do work, discover that sign-offs were not official, and the wheel kept spinning. Our cash flow dried up and we were in a trap.

At another project in the UK we had been starting at risk, months in advance. The big issue was not that we worked on the basis of a word, but how long it dragged on. After many months without cash flow relief, this started causing serious stress on all team members.

As I experienced in projects in the U.S., Canada and the UK, this can be aggravated when a systems integrator (SI) is involved. At that point these kinds of project challenges cascade down the hierarchy. Communication is not forthcoming, and motivations are questioned.

Nothing of the above has anything to do with any specific work component. If there are issues, then they need to be addressed. If work needs to get done, it needs to get done.

But there needs to be an alignment. You, your internal team members, your consultants, your other contractors - all interests need to be aligned and formalities should not get in the way of anybody's performance in a project. Don't let distrust and questioning of motivations creep into a project. Usually this happens involuntarily. But it does happen.

In more than half of the dozens of SAP-Primavera projects I have been involved in I encountered one of two situations, and sometimes both:

1. The server infrastructure is established late, impacting the project schedule, or
2. External service providers are kept waiting or working at risk.

Address them, and make sure the interests of all parties are properly aligned!

How to Prevent the Pitfall:

- Define all provisioning steps before official project kickoff.
- Be clear about the project parameters, as outlined in the above Step 2.
- Don't start the project until contractual and procurement logistics are sorted out and formalized.
- Consider significant delays if contractual matters are not sorted out as envisioned.
- Have a sponsor who can make things happen to prevent delays.

#15. Performing a POC with the Wrong Tools

The Problem: Trying to evaluate EPC's capabilities by using the out-of-the-box sample workflow and mappings

Every once in a while I encounter interesting interpretations of the words "proof of concept" or "POC". Often I wonder whether this is a formal process, or something imposed to the team by management, rather than a real nose-in-the-ground fact finding mission. The big problem with that is that it can lead to drawing the wrong conclusions.

Two variations of impractical and straight-out risky POCs seem to be en vogue.

One is the POC defined as an installation of the out-of-the-box software package. Once the software is installed is when it gets tricky. Is that all you wanted to prove, that a software package can be installed? Or was your intention to prove that it can be installed in a specific technical setting, with a specific operating system, version of Primavera, database, etc.?

If the latter, then you did indeed prove something. If the former, that is more questionable. In any case, I hope you don't just stop there but validate success at least as the ability to demonstrate some real data flowing between the applications. In either case, the proof delivered by this exercise is that the technical infrastructure works and that the IT team is capable of installing it. No more.

The second type of POC is one that tries not just to install the out-of-the-box software package, but to hammer away at it and see to what degree it can deliver on specified functionality. In my experience this can quickly get off track. The biggest issue is that the out-of-the-box workflow and steps and mappings are extremely unlikely to render the advanced functionality that your business needs.

One then starts making modifications, and tweaks, and baby-steps, proving individual capabilities without addressing most of the big ticket items, like performance, error handling, concurrency, transfer controls, conditional updates, or project life-cycle reviews.

The result is a proof of concepts that you may have seen before, just more powerfully, in a demonstration of advanced solution templates that I or somebody else had shown you before. Why that was not enough for you to prove the underlying capability is beyond me. I am sure it had nothing to do with some of the other Myth's or Pitfalls that I listed herein.. Or did it?

The above is not to say that I don't like POCs, quite the opposite. I do see a high-value place for them, but not ring fenced with artificial limits of a sample workflow or sample mappings, or transfer controls so insufficient that they don't start addressing the most difficult questions of an implementation.

The POCs that have delivered most value for an implementation are those that help clarifying requirements as they simulate core and client-specific implementation processes. Like a real implementation it should use all tools available to deliver rapidly and as robustly as possible.

And, by the way, I have seen such "real" POCs successfully performed in either a client's environment, or hosted by outside experts. That part does not really matter. Unless you want to follow the above first interpretation of a POC, validating that the software can be installed.

How to Prevent the Pitfall:

Know exactly what you expect out of a POC. Proving a technical infrastructure as do-able may create some value but even that should not hold up your selection of a tool or a team. You gain the real value of a POC by proving a specific process, though. This reduces project risk since it can act as a gate. When performing such a POC do use the best tools and best experts out there. Don't try to re-invent the wheel. Focus on delivery and assessing capabilities, and don't limit yourself to using sample code or inexperienced personnel.

Addendum

Acronyms and Abbreviations

ABAP	Allgemeiner Berichts-Aufbereitungs Prozessor (Product of SAP)
API	Application Programming Interface
AS	Application Server
BAPI	Business Application Programming Interface (Product of SAP)
BP	British Petroleum (Company Name)
CATS	Cross-Application Time Sheet
CBS	Cost Breakdown Structure
CD	Compact Disc
CEI	Competitive Edge International (Company Name)
CIO	Central Information Officer
CO	Controlling (Product of SAP)
DSEX	Dates Set Externally (SAP Term)
EAI	Enterprise Application Integration
EAM	Enterprise Asset Management
ERP	Enterprise Resource Planning
ECC	Enterprise Central Component (Product of SAP)
ENC	Engineering and Construction
EPC	Enterprise Project Connection (Product of SAP), also: Engineer, Procure, Construct

EPS	Enterprise Project Structure
FF	Finish-Finish
FI	Financial Accounting (Product of SAP)
FS	Finish-Start
GC	General Contractor
HCM	Human Capital Management
HR	Human Resources
ID	Identifier
IM	Investment Management
IT	Information Technology
J2EE	Java Platform Enterprise Edition
JDK	Java Development Kit
JSF	Joint Strike Fighter
KPI	Key Performance Indicator
LDAP	Lightweight Directory Access Protocol
LAN	Local Area Network
LOE	Level of Effort
MM	Materials Management (Product of SAP)
MRP	Materials Requirements Planning
MRS	Multi-Resource Scheduling (Product of SAP)
MS	Microsoft
OMS	Outage Management Solution
P6	Primavera Project Planner Enterprise Version 6 (Product of Oracle)
PAM	Product Availability Matrix
PC	Personal Computer
PI	Process Integration

PM	Plant Maintenance (Product of SAP)
PMBOK	Project Management Book of Knowledge
PMO	Project Management Organization
PMI	Project Management Institute
PO	Purchase Order
POC	Proof of Concept, also: Percent of Completion
PPM	Project Portfolio Management
PRT	Production Resource and Tools
PS	Project System (Product of SAP)
PP	Production Planning (Product of SAP)
R&D	Research and Development
RAM	Random Access Memory
RFC	Remote Function Call
RFI	Request for Information
RFP	Request for Proposal
RFQ	Request for Quotation
ROI	Return on Investment
SAP	Systems, Applications, and Products in Dataprocessing (Company Name)
SF	Start-Finish
SI	Systems Integrator
SD	Sales and Distribution (Module of SAP)
SQL	Structured Query Language
SS	Start-Start
T&E	Time and Expense, also: T&M – Time and Materials
TCO	Total Cost of Ownership

TV	Television
UDF	User-defined Field
US	United States (of America), also: U.S.
USEA	United States Entergy Association
VPN	Virtual Private Network
WBS	Work Breakdown Structure
XI	Exchange Infrastructure (Product of SAP)
XSLT	Extensible Stylesheet Language Transformations

Index

"I'm still breathing."

Shane Mitchell